D1477511

ADVENTURE IN MY VEINS

Ex-Superintendent
ALLAN BRODIE, D.F.C.
with Roderick Grant

Adventure in My Veins

JARROLDS

JARROLDS PUBLISHERS (LONDON) LTD

178–202 Great Portland Street, London W1

AN IMPRINT OF THE HUTCHINSON GROUP

London Melbourne Sydney
Auckland Bombay Toronto
Johannesburg New York

First published 1968

*This book has been set in Bembo, printed in Great Britain
on Antique Wove paper by Anchor Press, and
bound by Wm. Brendon, both of Tiptree, Essex*

09 086440 9

To
those born with a wanderlust
and those who yearn for its
blessing

'There's a Legion that never was 'listed,
That carries no colours or crest,
But, split in a thousand detachments,
Is breaking the road for the rest.
Our fathers they gave us their blessing—
They taught us, and groomed us and crammed;
But we've shaken the Clubs and the Messes
To go and find out and be damned
                              (Dear boys!),
To go and get shot and be damned.'
Rudyard Kipling

Contents

Illustrations

Foreword

During his lifetime Allan Brodie has tackled, and been successful at, a variety of tasks. He has been a gamekeeper, uniformed police constable, Flying Squad detective sergeant, wrestler, pilot, bomb-aimer, athlete, jungle fighter— and now, once more, a gamekeeper again. From the age of twenty his life has been packed with danger and excitement, which he found in the streets of London, in the sky above Italy and North Africa, dropping by parachute to aid the Partisans in Yugoslavia and in the terrorist-infested jungles of Malaya during the toughest years of the Communist Emergency.

A decorated war hero his life has now turned circle and he has settled once more to work amid the purple-clad hills of Royal Deeside—the place he left as a youth to quest after adventure. He has led the sort of life that most men live only in their dreams. But out of the danger and excitement he has found contentment. His days of drama have helped him to come to terms with this mad, mad world in which we live. He can now enjoy the wonders of nature and the beauty of the countryside without feeling the urge to roam.

I first met Allan Brodie when I journeyed to his home to interview him for a newspaper article. As we talked it was not long before I realised that here was a story that begged to be told—a book that had to be written. In the months that followed we were to meet on many occasions, in his pleasant house in the lovely village of Aboyne, as he unfolded the story of his life—the story of a born adventurer.

I would like to express my thanks to the following people who have rendered assistance to me while writing this book: Dato L. C. Hoffman, Editor-in-Chief of the Straits Times Press (Malaya) Ltd., who made available photographs of the scene of the assassination of Sir Henry Gurney; Mr. David Tambyah, Singapore Editor of the *Malay Mail*, who put the file-room of the *Straits Times* building in Singapore at my disposal and, in addition to giving up some of his valuable time to answering my questions, was able, thanks to an alert memory, to pin-point items, thus saving me many hours of searching through back copies of the company's publications; Mr. M. Hutton, of the Malaysian High Commission in London; Mrs. George Bambridge, Rudyard Kipling's daughter; Methuen and Company Ltd., and the Macmillan Company of Canada for their permission to use the quotation from *The Lost Legion* by Rudyard Kipling. Last but by no means least, Senga Blackie for her labour in typing the manuscript and her husband, Ken, for his encouragement and valuable criticism.

RODERICK GRANT

Edinburgh

Ambush in the Afternoon

W HEN I saw the two men, dressed as police constables, dive headlong into the deep ditch at the side of the Malayan road, after stopping the Deputy Chief Police Officer's car, I knew I had been trapped in a terrorist ambush. As we accelerated, the guerillas opened up, sending a hail of bullets, from machine guns and rifles, ricocheting off the tarmac between the two cars. The instrument panel disintegrated in a dozen pieces as several slugs tore through the light bodywork of my Austin A.40 and I looked in the mirror, expecting retaliation from the eight special constables travelling in our escorting armoured truck. To my horror the vehicle was not behind me. We were on our own . . .

It was August 1951, and I was having breakfast in my bungalow at Serdang, in South Kedah, when the signal came through: 'Deputy Chief Police Officer arriving this morning. Prepare for transfer.' The message brightened the start to my day—I had spent several months in Serdang and taken no liking to the place. The work of obtaining information about Communist terrorist movements and the attempts to trap those who supplied them with food had grown tedious and frustrating. No one would talk and the guerillas had grown elusive. The thought of a change to more attractive surroundings was a pleasant one.

Bobby Hicks arrived shortly after 10 p.m., having taken the long route, from the headquarters in Alor Star, via Bukit Mertajam and Parit Buntar, crossing the Sungai

Krian by the hand-poled ferry to Bandar Bahru. His news was good—I was to be posted to Padang Besar, a small village on the Malay/Thailand border, as Superintendent in charge of Frontier Security and Customs.

After lunch and an inspection of my men and station the Deputy Chief was ready to go. As he intended making a call at the police station at Kulim, while en route for Alor Star, the decision was made to dispense with the ferry and take the shorter but more dangerous route on the narrow twisting road, which ran through a series of deep gorges and patches of dense jungle.

I issued orders for our semi-armoured vehicle, with a driver and eight special constables, to act as escort for our two private cars. We set off with Bobby in the lead, my car following, with my Chinese orderly sitting beside me in the front seat, and the armoured truck fifty yards behind. The journey through the Serdang terrain was uneventful and we were able to maintain a steady 35 m.p.h. as we crossed over into the Kulim district.

Glancing in my mirror, I saw the dust rising behind me, partly obliterating the escorting vehicle. The road began to twist and turn as we entered some deep cuttings with intermittent areas of rubber trees on one side and thick jungle on the other.

Six hundred yards from the Padang Terap police post, as the road passed through a gorge with the jungle so thick that it cut out the harsh rays of the hot afternoon sun, two smartly dressed policemen stepped out from the trees and held up their hands in a signal to halt.

I saw Bobby brake and bring his car to a halt. Changing gear and slowing down, I had almost brought my car to a standstill twenty yards behind his vehicle when, instead of saluting and moving forward to speak to the Deputy Chief, the two men threw themselves off the road and rolled into the ditch.

Bobby's reaction was instantaneous with my own. Crashing the gears, we stepped on the accelerator pedals and our cars shot forward. The guerillas, hiding in the dense undergrowth, opened fire and the bullets sprayed across the road. I heard several strike my car and saw the speedometer and other instruments vanish as the dashboard was ripped apart. As it dawned on me that we had no armoured truck to return the fire, I thought: 'This is it, Brodie. You've asked for this for a long time. Now your number really is up!'

My orderly dived on the floor of the car and I heard him shout. I had no time to look to see if he had been hit. With a vicious wrench my car swerved to the left, as the machinegun and rifle bullets ripped the rubber from the front nearside tyre. I hauled on the steering wheel, trying desperately to correct the swing, and felt a searing pain as a bullet passed through the door beside me and ripped the front of my right trouser leg, furrowing the skin on my shin. Punching a hole in the back of the orderly's shirt, which billowed upwards as he lay prostrate on the floor, the slug slammed through the passenger door and was gone again.

The A.40 slewed all over the road as the tortured rubber was swept away by the rough surface. A volley of shots hit the rear and with a loud bang the offside tyre burst, hauling the car back on an even course. Bobby's car was now out of sight and round a bend in the road and, as I gained speed, a fresh hail of slugs ripped along the tail, smashing the rear window into fragments.

Careering along on the rims of two wheels I passed out of the ambush area, followed by a fusillade of shots whining into the grass beside the car and rattling off the rear. Bumping and clattering on the hard surface, I did not decrease speed until I swung into the barbed-wire compound behind the police post. As I brought the A.40 to a standstill and my orderly raised his head from the floor I saw Bobby being helped from his car. He had been hit in two places and blood poured profusely from wounds in his buttocks and a gash caused by a bullet as it had passed through his right heel.

As one of the local constables tried to staunch the flow of blood the armoured vehicle thundered up the road. The red-faced driver jumped out and rushed up to me to explain that he had been held up by engine trouble. I was about to inform him that we had encountered an ambush when he saw Bobby being laid face downwards on a blanket.

'The Chief . . . he has been shot?' he asked, with a puzzled expression on his face.

I quickly told him of the ambush and although he had only been minutes behind us, the terrorists had either disappeared from the scene or refrained from opening fire on the armoured vehicle when it passed by. We rushed Bobby, in the armoured truck, to the hospital in Kulim, but after a quick examination the doctors advised that he should be transported to Alor Star, where better facilities were available. My own wound was nothing—little more than a graze—and a tight bandage was all that was necessary.

I returned to Padang Terap the following day and on examining the cars found fifteen bullet holes in the Deputy Chief's vehicle and over twenty in my own. One bullet, no doubt ricocheting from the road, had gone straight through the petrol tank of my A.40 about half an inch above the base. I had indeed been lucky that the police post had been so close.

A police platoon which had gone to the ambush spot found prepared positions for over thirty men and masses of empty bullet cases, from automatic weapons and rifles, littering the undergrowth. Although they had done their best to follow a trail, this had proved useless due to the maze of paths in the jungle, which were used daily by rubber tappers on their way to and from the nearby plantations.

Three months later a terrorist camp was found in the Kulim area. This had been hastily abandoned on the approach of a security patrol and among the items left lying around were a number of documents. One described the killing of two Europeans in an ambush at the exact time and in the same place that Bobby and I had our narrow escape. Who was kidding whom . . . I had just celebrated my thirty-ninth birthday and never felt more alive.

B

2

A Pocketful of Mischief

I WAS nearly fourteen years old when I saw, for the first time, in 1926, the blue-heather hills and the pine forests of Royal Deeside. I drank in huge gulps of the pure, clean air and looked over the woods across the valley to the snow-capped peak of the 3,070 ft. Mount Keen, which stands, stark and grim, like some relic from the volcanic age. How was I, a raw youth, fresh from school, to know that this scene would remain imprinted on my mind—as a negative superimposes itself upon sensitive photographic paper—to come to life again, time after time, in the streets of Soho, in the fuselage of a Wellington bomber and in the terrorist-infested jungles of the Malayan Peninsula.

My father, Peter, a gamekeeper, as generations of Brodies had been before him, had obtained a job as a deerstalker on Glentanar Estate, in Aberdeenshire. When I entered the world on August 8, 1912, my parents were living at Coull, at the head of Loch Fyne in Argyll, but during my early childhood we lived both in Glencoe and in the Borders. All the time we were in the south of Scotland my father nursed a secret desire to return once more to the Highlands, and from the first day he told the family we were to move from our home in the Cheviot Hills and go north to Aboyne I could scarcely control my excitement. My two sisters, Jean and Christina, and I had listened often to my father's stories of his beloved Highland mountains. We had heard of the stags, the wild cats and the golden eagles and been told of

6

the powerful salmon to be found in the rushing torrents of the mountain rivers.

For us the world of stories was about to become a living reality and I was only sure I was not dreaming the whole thing when we reached the 'heart' of the Glentanar Estate, about five miles from Aboyne village.

The 'heart' was a village in its own right. It composed of the Mansion House, as it was referred to by everybody, in which lived the laird, Lord Glentanar; the stable-yard, which consisted of a row of houses, stables and garages, which had been used some years before as coach-houses; and a recreation hall, built of cedar. It was in this building that dances and whist drives were held during the long, dark winter months.

There was a house for the farm manager, farm workers' houses and a collection of granite buildings to house scores of cattle during winter. These cows supplied the milk for the entire population of the estate.

A little further away was the head gamekeeper's house, the young gamekeepers' bothy, four other employees' houses, and finally a substantial granite building holding dog kennels and boilers for cooking the meat with which the animals were fed. I was most impressed. From those early days and right to the present time Glentanar estate has been a first-class model in its general layout, living conditions, recreation and general interest in the welfare of its employees. But we were not to stay in the village. A deerstalker, by the very nature of his job, must be near to the hills and corries frequented by his charges. We journeyed on for another five miles until we reached the door of Eitnach House, which was to be my parents' home for the next thirteen years.

It is difficult to describe the feeling of joy in my heart that first night as I helped my father and mother to move our belongings into the house. Perhaps, really, I wasn't of much assistance to them. I was too enthralled by the country-side around me, and in particular by the sight of a huge herd of deer—there must have been four hundred—feeding out from the forest. I had fallen in love for the very first time.

My parents' first thoughts were that I should go back to school again—this time to the school in Aboyne. But I had other ideas. I had never really liked school and all the trappings of learning. For me the only life was an outdoor one—the only subjects I wished to learn more about were the hunting of a stag and the art of luring a salmon from a river.

All the same my schooldays had been happy ones. They were days spent in the company of boys and girls like myself. Children with mischief in our minds but prepared to accept punishment when it came—as it usually did more often than not. The first teacher I had was Miss Knight, who had sole charge of the tiny country school at Hounam, in the Borders. She was a stout, slow-moving person, but good-natured and kindly. It took a great deal to make her angry, but when this did happen her means of retaliation were swift and severe. Many's a day I have returned home from school with my hands numb from the blows received from the hefty leather strap she used to punish the wrong-doers.

The most severe hiding I ever had from her occurred during a lunch-break. I was walking past her kitchen and could not resist having a look through the window. Miss Knight was hard at work, making her supply of jam. There on top of the fire was a large jelly-pan with the mouth-watering scent of blackcurrant jam wafting from it. I crept away and informed two pals. It would be the height of fun, we decided, to drop something down the chimney and into the jam. A piece of turf would do the trick. I would do the 'bombing'.

I arranged that my pals would hang around in the vicinity of the window. They were to signal to me to drop the turf when they saw the unfortunate Miss Knight leave the vicinity of the fire. This was to prevent her from getting burned in the chaos which was to follow, we hoped.

I dug a sizable piece of turf and, after a struggle, climbed to the top of the two-storey house. Hanging on to the stone chimney with one hand, I eased the turf over the edge. It dropped down into the black opening and was gone from view in a matter of seconds. My two pals only waited long enough to see a great cloud of soot burst up from the region of the fireplace. This was enough for them—they fled.

Miss Knight, who dashed to the fireplace to investigate, found the jam splattered everywhere and soot clinging to the curtains and furniture of her once spotless kitchen. She was quick to realise that the destruction of her jam was no act of God but more likely the Devil at work, in the shape of a small boy. She rushed from the house bent on revenge.

At this point I was in mid-air between roof and ground. I dropped down to land almost at her feet. Quick as a flash she caught hold of me by the collar and I was marched double-quick into the little classroom. There I stood, as manfully as I could, while the irate Miss Knight exerted all her energy into delivering twenty wallops of the strap to my hands.

This was bad enough, but the punishment did not end with Miss Knight. A letter was sent to my parents informing them of my dastardly deed. I had never seen my father so angry before. Putting the letter on the table he went to a cupboard and produced a thick razor strop. It is sufficient to say that I could neither sit down nor hold anything in my hands for days after this.

Like most of my pals at school I never once felt any resentment towards the teachers who strapped me. As far as I was concerned I almost always deserved it. I was quick to realise that if I was caught acting mischievously then punishment must follow. If I was not caught—I had been lucky and that was that.

Even at Oxnam School, a senior elementary school in Roxburghshire, which I attended when I was ten years old, I was unable to keep out of mischief. The headmaster, Mr. Patterson, was a strict disciplinarian, but even he became exasperated by my pranks. He ceased using his strap on my hands—instead he chose a particularly nasty cane which he seemed to keep for my exclusive use.

One day while walking to school I saw an adder in the grass beside the path. Picking it up, I popped it into a paper bag which I used to carry my sandwiches to be eaten at the lunch-time break.

The headmaster's classroom was empty when I reached school. I nipped in smartly and, lifting the lid of Mr. Patterson's desk, opened the paper bag and released the adder among a collection of attendance registers, ink bottles and pens and pencils. I dropped the lid back into place and slipped out. I kept my mouth shut when I met my friends— by this time I knew the folly of telling others of mischief just accomplished. A few minutes later I was back in the room again attending morning prayers with the rest of the pupils.

A hymn was sung and heads were bowed in prayer. All the time Mr. Patterson stood behind his desk, one eye on the bible, the other on the back of the room, ready to spot any troublemaker.

The religious proceedings over, the headmaster's next task was to mark the register of those present and absent. He placed the bible at the side of the desk and opened the lid to reach for the register. It was to be many years before I was able to see a comparable look of horror on any man's face. He took a step backwards, colliding with a chair on the way, his face white, as he saw the two-foot-long snake coiled up ready to strike. It was very angry and showed it by hissing noisily and moving its head around from side to side.

There were shouts of astonishment from the pupils who could see and from the others less fortunate there was a craning of necks in an attempt to see the reason for the headmaster's strange behaviour. The adder—still hissing loudly—tried to get over the edge of the desk. This brought Mr. Patterson to life again. Still hypnotised by the adder's cold stare, he shouted: 'There's a snake in my desk,' to be greeted by a mixed chorus of laughter from the boys and shrieks from the girls.

I felt the fun had gone on long enough. I dashed up to the desk and with a heavy ruler killed the offending reptile. The headmaster was profuse in his thanks—his gratitude knew no bounds as he praised me in front of the assembled pupils and talked of the 'brave deed' I had done.

When I left Oxnam to go north with my family I knew the time had come to make a break from school. In a man-to-man talk with my father I told him I wanted nothing more from life than to be as good a gamekeeper as he was. I must have sounded convincing. He gave his approval and the next month I started work as a kennel boy at Glentanar. As this involved feeding and looking after dogs at all times of the day and night, I moved from my parents' house to the bothy in the estate village. There I shared my new home with three others—John McPherson, the laird's piper and ponyman; Willie Espie and Alistair Ford.

My boss, the head gamekeeper, Peter Strang, was one of the most capable and efficient gamekeepers I have ever met. Right from the start he took a personal interest in teaching me to shoot and carry out my other duties, which included rearing wild pheasants and wild duck, trapping vermin, such as stoats and foxes, and the care and 'breaking-in' of dogs.

I had picked up quite a few tips on many of these things from my father when I was a small boy, but it was Peter Strang who put the finer touches on my ability to carry out these tasks.

I felt ten foot tall when, on my fifteenth birthday, he appointed me as a fully fledged under-gamekeeper. Willie Espie left the estate and I took over his job. In turn my old job, as kennel boy, went to a tall gangling youth called Eddie McPhail, also from Argyll. We were to be inseparable friends for the next four years.

In those days I was paid the princely sum of £1 10s. per

week—at the end of each three-monthly period. Both Eddie and I were bad financial managers and many times we found we had little money left after the first two weeks had elapsed. John McPherson came to the rescue and instead of each man fending for himself we agreed to pool our resources. This led to the allocation of duties and we each took turns of being cook and general provider for the household. There was always the meat of the deer—venison—to be had, at least from August to January, and for the rest of the year, when we could not afford to buy meat, there were rabbits and hares aplenty.

One of my favourite sports is fishing. It always has been —right from the age of seven—and still is today. In a way I can thank Peter Strang for this—it was he who furthered my interest by teaching me the art of fly-fishing.

Well do I remember the first day of February 1928, when I went with him to the River Dee, one of the greatest salmon rivers in Britain. There, at the fishing hut at Waterside Pool, he fitted together the pieces of an eighteen-foot greenheart rod, equipped with a great metal reel and heavy sunk line. After tying on the cast and a three-inch Mar Lodge fly he started to show me the elementary principles of fly-fishing.

I got to grips with the general idea of things fairly quickly, but the strain of switching the rod back and fore through the air, between each cast, then holding it as the fly travelled through the water, nearly broke my back. At the end of the day we had nothing to show for our labours.

Next day I was back at the river again—the muscles of my arms and my back aching. I fished down the pool carefully, as instructed by the watchful head gamekeeper, and was just nearing the tail when I felt a fierce pull on the line. The reel began to scream. I held the rod-tip high, hung on as if glued to the wood, and started to play the fish.

Up and down the pool it went, sometimes running swiftly and deep in the water. On other occasions the salmon would leap high into the air and with a mighty flick of its tail, turn a somersault, only to crash back into the water in a cloud of spray—still firmly hooked.

After fifteen minutes of such behaviour the fish began to tire and I sighed with relief as I brought it to the bank, where it moved listlessly against the stones—all fight gone from its powerful body. Thanks to Peter it was soon on the bank and I looked down on the lifeless body of my first trophy from the river—a silvery, wonderfully proportioned eighteen-pound salmon, fresh from the sea. Without wasting a moment I was back, wielding the rod once more, all thoughts of sore backs and aching muscles buried for ever at the back of my mind.

In the early 1930's Glentanar Estate was hit by a plague amongst the sheep and cattle. Every beast was covered with thousands of ticks—minute parasites which burrowed under the skin and sucked the blood of the unfortunate beasts. Most of the animals were reduced to skin and bone and many died.

The deer were blamed as the carriers of these parasites and orders were issued that many would have to be shot. For weeks after this I spent long, hard days on the moors, shooting as many as possible and transporting them back to the larders for skinning. This was the time of the great depression and most of the deer carcases were sent to the worst-hit of the mining areas. It was wholesale slaughter but a job that had to be done.

Never before had I been given the opportunity of such rifle practice and as a result I was soon a proficient shot. There were to be many times in Malaya when I was to bless these weeks of mass-hunting, for they enabled me to shoot fast, and with great accuracy, and to stalk, quietly, after unsuspecting prey.

By now I was nineteen and starting to realise that there was a larger world outside. John McPherson was quick to sense that my horizons were widening and on his advice I attended evening classes to study English, mathematics and geography. A few months later, with this fresh knowledge aflame inside me, I felt the pull of the wanderlust. But what should I do and where should I go? I asked myself. I had to have a job which offered me plenty of variety and, if possible, excitement. I wanted something I could come to grips with —something into which I could get my teeth.

I turned to the police force and, making use of the additional grammar acquired at the evening classes, wrote a letter to the recruiting officer of the London Metropolitan Force. The reply came with instructions to report to my local police station for educational tests and a medical examination. For a couple of weeks after these had been completed I waited for the postman to bring word from London. Eventually it came—I was to make myself available for a further education test and medical examination at New Scotland Yard on January 2, 1933. If successful I would immediately enter the police training school, said the letter; if I failed I would be given a railway ticket for my return to Aboyne.

When I handed over my bicycle to the local stationmaster and asked him to look after it for me for a few days I was sure I would be back. I was positive that the men in London would not want me for their great police force. After all, I thought, there must be thousands of young men eager and willing to join the ranks of the police.

It would be twenty-four years before I tramped over my beloved hills again, a gun under my arm and a dog at my heel. The tiny piece of cardboard which I held in my hand, as I boarded the train, was to be my ticket for the first stage of adventure round the world.

3

'... Through Streets Broad and Narrow'

To my immense relief, and surprise, the Metropolitan Police decided to have me for their ranks. And it took them exactly one day to make up their minds. But before that day was out I was to realise that the discipline was strict and that the sergeants chosen to enforce it on the raw recruits would stand no nonsense.

At Peel House, the Metropolitan Police Training School, along with six other lads from the North of England, I was given a thorough lecture on the rules and regulations. We were then shown to our rooms. They were really cubicles, one to each man—cheerless-looking places, with the bare minimum of furniture, consisting of a bed, small table, one chair and a wardrobe.

This was to be home for ten weeks during which I was taught every aspect of police work that could possibly be covered by lectures. There was also drill one hour per day, Sundays excepted, when Sergeant Hinchcliff ruled his sweating recruits with a rod of iron. This was by far the most unpopular part of the recruit training. Our physical training instructor, Sergeant Bissell, was one of the finest wrestlers in the country and as I showed interest in this line of sport he soon had me enrolled in his section.

Eventually we moved on to Class One and the day of the final examinations. Everyone passed and in the evening our postings came through. With young Charlie Ottaway I found myself drafted to 'N' Division with the number 348. I would be paid £3 a week.

Next day at Stoke Newington police station Superintendent Hunt, better known as 'Daddy Hunt', put us wise
to the many pitfalls and temptations we were likely to
encounter as young, green policemen on the beat. If we
kept our noses clean no harm would come to us, he advised.

My new home was to be the section house at the rear of
the police station and a right old gloomy place it turned out
to be. There was a basement where our lockers and uniforms
were housed and a canteen and toilets. On the ground floor
there was a dining-room and lounge while above, for three
floors, were the sleeping quarters—again each man occupying a tiny cubicle.

Section-house life was far removed from the essence of
home comfort. We had one meal a day, provided for us,
and for the rest of the day were expected to cook for
ourselves. There was a big black range in the mess hall and
an ample supply of cooking utensils.

The rules governing our life there were many and
varied, the worst hardship being compelled to be back in
our quarters by midnight. This childish regulation was
broken more often than any of the others.

Unfortunately the sergeant-in-charge was wise to every
trick in the book, but we were not long in discovering that
he did not check on the whereabouts of the inhabitants every
night. Invariably we were able to make a stealthy entry over
the high wall and gate, which was locked on the witching
hour of midnight, and climb up the fire escape into our
rooms.

The following Monday morning at 8 a.m. Charlie and I
reported to St. Anne's Road police station, and for two
weeks experienced policemen acted as chaperons. Their
only source of conversation was running down the force
and telling us what bloody fools we had been to join up in
the first place.

My heart pounded with mixed feelings of pride and fear
when I first emerged from the station to go on the beat
alone. Dutifully I pounded the pavements at regulation

pace, not quite realising what I was looking for, and too scared when I thought of all the things that could happen should I put one foot wrong and wrongfully arrest someone.

Several times people hurried in my direction and as they approached I scanned their faces, trying to make up my mind whether it was robbery, murder or rape they were about to report. To my relief they all passed by.

It took me a month to get to grips with my first law-breaker and the trouble started in Green Lanes, Harringay—a busy shopping area. As I turned into the street I saw the usual disorderly collection of costermongers' barrows lined up on my side of the beat. One barrow was right on the corner of a side street partially blocking the flow of traffic. I dithered around for a few minutes, hoping it would vanish before my eyes, but no such luck. Plucking up courage, I stepped over and asked the barrow boy to move the offending cart.

My order released from him a string of Cockney abuse. He told me to grow some whiskers on my chin before chucking my weight about. His hysterical voice attracted the attention of the shoppers and in next to no time a large crowd had gathered—no doubt relishing the sight of a fool being made of a rookie copper.

Sticking my chest out, I told the barrow boy that if he didn't move he would find himself in the police station. More abuse this time—accompanied by much waving of the arms. He really was enjoying himself. Finally I could stand his ranting no longer and told him I was going to arrest him for causing an obstruction. Pointing to the barrow, I told him to push it down the street to the police station.

He was having none of this. To cheering from the crowd he announced: 'If you're going to nick me, copper, you can push the bloody barrow yourself.'

There was nothing for it but to do just that. I have never felt such a fool. Here was I, in uniform, pushing a heavy brute of a costermonger's barrow, loaded with fruit, half a mile to the police station with the ever-gibing owner walking beside me, informing amazed passers-by that it was kind of the police force to supply him with an assistant. I could have throttled him.

Next day he was fined 5s. From that day on I never arrested another barrow boy.

Tragedy struck with a vengeance a few months later when I was on duty near a church which stood close to the police station. I watched the arrival of the gaily decorated cars and the occupants lining up on both sides of the path leading to the door to await the arrival of the bride. Eventually she came and with her father walked up to the church.

All of a sudden the sound of women screaming cut through the air and the crowd on the path started to mill around. I ran across and in the centre of a circle of horrified wedding guests found a young man lying just inside the door. He was writhing around, moaning, and seemed to be in great pain.

Someone shouted that he had drunk some poison. Picking him up in my arms, I carried him down the street and into the station. Laying him on the floor in the charge-room, I ran to the first-aid box for some white chalk. When I returned I saw, to my horror, that the substance he was vomiting up was burning a hole in the wooden floor. Trying desperately to remember the first-aid training from my Peel House days, I ground up the white chalk and forced some down his throat.

An ambulance arrived, summoned by the station officer, and I set off with the man on the way to hospital. He kept lashing out as his body was racked by a fresh spasm of pain and before we reached the hospital he died. When I made inquiries later in the day I found that he had been jilted by the bride-to-be. Swallowing poison was his revenge for her marrying another man.

After a year in the uniformed branch I spoke to the local C.I.D. chief about my chances of joining his department. Four months later I was interviewed by the Divisional

Detective Inspector and soon found myself classed as an 'Aid to C.I.D.'

Our hours were long and our duties varied, with many tedious stints of keeping people and premises under observation. Sometimes this type of work would last for days on end and often with negative results.

A regular port of call was the famous Caledonian Market. Normally a cattle market, it was used by stallholders for two days of the week. From these stalls you could buy anything, from the proverbial needle to an anchor. I must have made dozens of arrests in this place—mostly pickpockets.

While at the Kentish Town police station I met Sid Dance, who was an absolute marvel when it came to catching thieves. His instinct was unerring. It was Sid who showed me the methods used by different classes of criminals and pointed out the ways in which one could detect them. One typical lesson of his was how to detect pickpockets and shoplifters.

Firstly the detective must take up an unobtrusive position in a crowd, facing the most dense part, and then scan the faces of those before him. It is an easy matter to pick out the pickpockets as their eyes dart from one side to the other, prior to stealing from a stall, counter or shopping bag.

With pickpockets there may be anything from a lone wolf to up to six operating as a highly organised gang. The single pickpocket has to be really adept, as he has to combine the 'push-up', which usually consists of barging rather heavily into the selected victim, who has already been 'drummed' (i.e. the pocket which contains the wallet or roll of notes has been located) with the actual theft.

The pickpocket usually carries a newspaper, carefully folded in half, or a flat parcel or raincoat, folded over the left forearm. Any of these acts as a 'smother' and is pushed up in front of the victim's face while the right hand is inserted into the inside jacket pocket.

All these actions are done while on the move as the pickpocket forces his way through the crowd. When the 'smother' is pushed in front of the victim's face his attention is immediately drawn to it because it is the heaviest and most obvious point of contact while the slight pull of the wallet being removed goes unnoticed.

With a gang, the method differs in that two or more pickpockets barge into the victim, thus lending themselves better concealment from the rest of the crowd. The gang always have a 'minder', especially when there are crowds at bus stops, railway stations or on crowded trains. These, together with dog and horse-racing tracks, are the pickpockets' favourite stomping grounds.

Whenever a wallet is stolen it is passed to the 'minder'—usually a well-dressed woman—who leaves the crowd at the first available opportunity to go to a ladies' toilet or some other secluded spot. There the contents of the wallet are removed. It is then discarded, along with any other incriminating evidence. The woman then makes her way to some prearranged meeting place where the gang can sort out their loot.

Pickpockets working in gangs are the most difficult to convict. With a 'minder' operating and the stolen goods being whisked away so speedily, should the theft be noticed, nothing relating to it can be found on the actual persons involved and they get off scot free.

I was still at Kentish Town when the Mosley riots broke out. My first sample of trouble was at a meeting held in a side street off Kentish Town Road. Sir Oswald Mosley was the principal speaker. Dozens of uniformed and plainclothes men were drafted in from the surrounding divisions to deal with any outbreak of trouble.

I was working with Johnny McMillan, a tough, wiry lad from Benbecula, in the Outer Hebrides. We were briefed to mingle with the crowd and take up positions near any group of potential trouble-makers. With our short truncheons in our pockets we moved warily through the crowds gathered on either side of the street.

I noticed a large group of young Jews standing on the kerbside. They looked rough, tough and angry and well worth watching. One took a set of knuckledusters from his pocket and fitted them on to his right hand.

A few minutes later Mosley's car started to drive along the street and as it approached there was a fantastic uproar from the anti-Mosleyites. The group of Jews moved forward into the roadway. As they did so one of them turned and spotted Johnny and me.

He shouted: 'Look out . . . there's two bloody coppers in plain clothes behind us, lads!'

Another took up the cry, yelling wildly: 'Down with the coppers! Smash Mosley's bodyguard!'

In one fell movement they were attacking us. There were other weapons besides knuckledusters and they used them with a vengeance. I succeeded in flattening two of them and injuring several others. Eventually they broke off the engagement, but the fight was not gone from them.

Within seconds they had descended on a crowd of East End toughs acting as Mosley's official bodyguards. This time the battle was long and bloody. Fists, chains, boots, knuckledusters, steel bars were the weapons and it was only the arrival of the mounted police, wielding their long truncheons to great effect, that saved the day for law and order.

Ringed by mounted and uniformed police Sir Oswald's car was escorted away from the scene and the meeting cancelled. He had not uttered one word, yet an entire street was in chaos.

Johnny and I picked up two Jewish casualties, who had been trampled on by the mob as well as being knocked out, and took them to the station. The charge-room was littered with battered bodies. The final count was twenty, but there must have been scores more licking their wounds that night.

These meetings continued in Kentish Town, Ridley Road, Dalston, and the East End of London and each time the violence increased. There were strong anti-Jewish feelings

C

among the working classes and hundreds rallied to Mosley's cause. Many of his followers had genuine feelings, but for the most it was an undisciplined, unruly mob that followed him around, eager for the spark that would fire the attack.

Sir Oswald was a skilful orator and within minutes of starting his speech would have his followers worked into a state of near frenzy.

The final display of his campaign was to be a motorcade led by him along Mile End Road, then into Commercial Road, terminating in a meeting in one of the side streets.

Hundreds of policemen were on duty and almost every mounted policeman in the Metropolitan area was called in. Once again my task was to mingle with the crowds.

I was a good way up the Mile End Road when I saw the cars forming up. They started to approach slowly, preceded by twelve mounted policemen and flanked by many more, with another twelve taking up the rear. Other policemen struggled grimly in an attempt to hold back the mass of people pressing forward from the pavements.

I was puzzled because of the strange air of quietness that hung over the crowds. There must have been thousands of people present but little noise was evident.

The peace was finally shattered by a shout of 'Smash Mosley', which rang out loud and clear from some point at the rear of the crowd. The mob pressed forward. The policemen linked hands and arms and leaned backwards, but at point after point the mob broke through, shouting and cursing.

Thousands of marbles were thrown in the paths of police horses. A number slipped and fell, pitching their riders at the feet of the now hysterical demonstrators. The procession came to a standstill and a pitched battle ensued.

I was struck many times, but dished out far more blows in reply. It was impossible to arrest anyone in the heat of the fray—all one could do was fight back as hard as possible.

Gradually we began to regain control and one tough swung at me with a rubber cosh loaded with lead. Fortunately I saw it coming and ducked out of the way, receiving only a glancing blow to the side of the head. I retaliated with a hefty chop from my much-used truncheon, which put him out of action.

When the mob was dispersed and a tally made there were numerous hospital cases on both sides—the ratio: four thugs to one policeman. Fifty arrests were made.

All such meetings were barred from that date.

Eighteen months later I was advanced to detective constable and posted to C.I.D. 'G' Division, a difficult area to police, which embraced City Road, Islington, Old Street, Dalston and Commercial Street. For the next three years, while I operated from the stations at Shepherdess Walk, City Road, Old Street and Commercial Street, there were not many dull days.

On my arrival at Shepherdess Walk police station I reported to Divisional Detective Inspector Salisbury, a man of vast experience, most of whose C.I.D. knowledge was gained in the East End. He was abrupt in speech and did not waste time beating about the bush. In short, curt sentences he told me what was expected of a young detective, of the long hours I would have to work and the many distasteful duties I would be called upon to perform.

I then met the rest of my colleagues, headed by Detective Inspector Arthur Davies, a true Cockney. His favourite advice was always 'cop a statement'. It was certainly a wise procedure, especially when the person being interviewed had signed the document after having read it over. Poor Arthur, his advice rebounded on him at a later stage when, as a member of the Murder Squad, he charged a man with little evidence other than a signed statement which, later, the accused denied having made, and the charge was unceremoniously thrown out at the magistrates' court.

There were seven of us altogether and, although the hours were long and often tedious, there was always plenty of fun, especially among the detective constables, who were John Gosling, a farmer's son from Manningtree, Essex,

George Burton, a Cockney, and Jock Easson, from the Borders.

There was a great deal of practical joking and the main victim was an elderly Detective Sergeant—Bill Bowler. True to his name, he always wore a bowler hat. On several occasions he would rush to get out of the office on a case, only to find that his bowler was nailed to the desk. He would always appear to be extremely annoyed, but secretly he enjoyed the fun—no doubt he found it a change from the normally staid atmosphere of a police station.

But it was not all fun and games and my first encounter with gang warfare happened when I was in this district.

I had not been there long before I found myself alone on duty one Sunday. I received a telephone call informing me of a gang fight outside the Macclesfield Arms pub in City Road. The agitated caller spoke of about twenty people being involved. I went through to the station officer, and told him what was going on and asked if I could have the police van. He was well used to dealing with such matters and told me calmly: 'There's no hurry, lad. You will get the van and I will send a couple of uniformed boys with you but we'll give them about ten minutes, then go up and collect the bodies.'

I hung around, impatiently, until the transport was arranged—then with two uniformed constables set off to the Macclesfield Arms. In the forecourt of the pub a spectacular fight was in progress. There were between eighteen and twenty people scrapping with each other and four men were lying on the pavement.

The contestants were armed with a variety of weapons, ranging from clubs with nails driven through them to a fearsome-looking Turkish scimitar brandished by a swarthy Scotsman known as Jock Wilson. When the police van stopped, the fight broke up and there was a scramble to get into several cars parked near the pub. We ran after the men and I managed to grab one, who was known to me as Micky. The others managed to escape, but not before I recognised the two brothers Peters, who ran an Islington gang, and Jock, who was a member of the Macclesfield Street gang.

I shoved Micky, who was bleeding from a gaping head wound, into the police van and had a look at the others lying around on the pavement. Some had multiple injuries but none appeared to be too seriously wounded. They too were bundled into the van and taken to the station. The Divisional Surgeon was called and after an hour of cleaning and stitching pronounced them as reasonably fit. All were charged with various offences and later the Peters brothers were arrested, as also was Jock.

It was discovered that a member of the Macclesfield Street gang was responsible for one of the Peters girls being pregnant and the battle had been a revenge carve-up. The Macclesfield mob had been drinking heavily in the pub when the Peters gang arrived in several cars, ready to fight. They called on their rivals to come outside and Dick Peters stood in the doorway, armed with a rubber cosh. Jock Wilson was first out and swung a mighty blow with his scimitar. Fortunately Dick Peters ducked, but it was a close shave as the crown was cut cleanly off his Anthony Eden hat.

For their part in the affray they all received sentences ranging from a few months up to one year in prison.

Not long after this I was almost ready to go off duty when the telephone rang—as it always seemed to do when the day's work was about to come to an end. A man, speaking from a telephone kiosk in Golden Square, Finsbury, shouted that a woman was being murdered in a nearby building.

When I got round I could hear screams coming from an office on the first floor and through the open window saw figures struggling together. With the police van driver I ran up the stairs and found the office door locked. It took us several minutes to force it in and when we entered the entire place looked like a butcher's shop. The walls, the furniture and floor were spattered with blood.

In a corner a woman was cowering and holding on to the wrist of a man who was standing over her with a large linoleum knife in his hand. I sprang at him and forced his arm up his back until he dropped the knife. He fought like a madman and although he was only slightly built seemed to have the strength of four men. Eventually he quieted down and the van-driver, who weighed about sixteen stone, sat on top of him.

I turned my attention to the woman, who was near to collapse. She was naked down to the waist and blood was pouring from some fearful gashes on her body. One breast was cut in half and one ear hung in ribbons.

While waiting for the ambulance I got a babbled version of what had happened. The man was her husband, she sobbed, and for some time he had suspected her of having an affair with someone in the office, where she was a cleaner.

He had crept in and openly accused her. She denied the accusations, but her husband had gone berserk with rage, produced the knife and started to slash her and rip off her clothing.

When the ambulance turned up the woman was placed on a stretcher and put inside. I also put the man, who was now calm and seemed in a deep state of shock, into the vehicle and went with them to the hospital. The surgeons spent six hours repairing the woman's wounds, which needed over 500 stitches. Her husband was later pronounced insane and sent to Broadmoor.

4

From Bombs to Bomb-sights

My next move was to Old Street police station and once again I found myself in a tough neighbourhood, which included Hoxton, the home ground of some of the hardest people in London. The pubs around Shoreditch were the favourite haunts of the 'whiz' or 'push-up' mobs (pickpocket gangs). I was fortunate to have stationed with me Ted Renson, who had been on the Flying Squad for fifteen years and knew every pickpocket registered in the files at New Scotland Yard. He was a great help to me because I was not long in realising that many of the people I would be dealing with would be pickpockets. In my opinion they were the lowest class of thief. Invariably it was the hard-working family man who was robbed of his earnings while having a pint with his mates before going home on a Friday night.

At this time there was a wave of thefts from railway delivery vans. These were horse-drawn vehicles and it was a simple matter for the thief to jump on the back and steal a package.

The favourite choice was nearly always a handy-sized five thousand or ten thousand package of cigarettes. Ted Renson and I were taken off all other duties to try to break up the thieving.

We contacted the railway police and secured the services of a good driver with a horse-drawn vehicle. On these vehicles the driver's seat was above the horse and the van was enclosed by a waterproof sheet, the back of which rolled up to allow loading or unloading. At the front of the van space we rigged up a dummy sheet inside and got a wooden bench to sit on. Once seated the false sheet was dropped, completely hiding us from view. There were peep-holes, however, so that we could keep a weather eye open for any likely clients.

Our bait was a ten thousand cigarette package, suitably loaded and displayed in a tempting position near the van's tailboard. Other packages were placed further into the van to make it look like a genuine load.

We knew of all the likely hangouts of the would-be thieves and decided to have a go along Shoreditch High Street and continue along Kingsland Road. We had only gone about a hundred yards up the High Street when we had our first bite.

Two youths were standing under a railway arch and as we passed they glanced at the rear of the van. Their eyes nearly popped out of their heads when they saw the package. With a quick glance up and down the street they trotted after the van, whipped the package off the tailboard and ran off down a side street. Ted and I gave chase and were round the corner and on top of them before they realised what had hit them. They gave in without a struggle and all the way to the station kept asking us where we had sprung from so quickly.

On another occasion we were plodding along Shoreditch High Street on the usual 'wagon patrol' when, as we passed a bus-stop, Ted, who was sitting on the nearside of the van, spotted three well-known pickpockets in the crowd. We signalled to Bill, our driver, to pull up just past the stop and, as he did so, a youth came out of the crowd and stood close to the van, taking great interest in the prominently dis-played package. He made no move towards it, probably because of the close proximity of so many people, but his intention was all too obvious.

A bus came along and there was considerable pushing

and shoving as people tried to get aboard. We watched the three pickpockets operating and although they could have boarded the bus, they turned back and once again mixed with the people who were waiting for the next vehicle. The same thing happened when it came along. We decided to try to make a double arrest, having seen enough to justify arresting the pickpockets. I signalled Bill, by thumping twice on the partition, to carry on down the street.

We had gone about fifty yards when the youth, who was still hanging around, nipped smartly up to the tailboard and removed the package. He walked away through a passageway and I jumped down and pursued him. When I caught hold of him he was so surprised that he surrendered immediately. As prearranged Ted went back to the bus stop and removed the three old pickpockets from the crowd. He told them to go round to Commercial Street police station and to wait there until he arrived. Equally amazed, the three old men set off without a murmur and Ted rejoined me. It was too much of a handful for me to cope with the package as well as the youth, so Ted carried the load.

When we arrived at the station the three pickpockets were sitting in the corridor, looking extremely dejected. They were charged and the following day were each sent to prison for three months. The van thief received six months.

We caught scores of thieves in a wide area of the East End while out with the railway vehicles, until we were spotted coming out of the van while in hot pursuit. Once was enough—the news of our method spread like wildfire and railway vans were strictly taboo for a long time.

At Commercial Street police station my superior was Detective Inspector Jock Black, a tough little Glaswegian. He was only five foot eight inches tall, but a first-class boxer and as hard as nails. Two other C.I.D. notables were Detective Sergeants Alec Howard and 'Nosher' Hearn, the latter being another top boxer.

One night Jock, Nosher and I were in the Princess Alice

pub chatting together over a few beers. The only other
occupant of the saloon bar was a man sitting near the fire.
Suddenly the peace was shattered by the sound of cars
drawing up outside. With a crash the door burst open.
Alfie Harris, the publican, shouted: 'Look out, they've got
chivs.'

There were ten in the gang, and the leader, a husky
individual, was holding a cut-throat razor, which he
brandished triumphantly above his head. The three of us
walked over to confront them.

Jock said: 'We are police officers. Get to hell out of here.'

The leader hesitated and we braced ourselves for trouble.
However, he obviously thought that discretion was the
better part of valour and replied: 'All right, guv. We were
after that bastard over there.'

He pointed to the man who sat beside the fire, his face a
sickly shade of grey.

He cursed the man once more and informed us: 'He
carved us out of our share in some gear.'

'Go on then, clear off . . . I'll not warn you again,' said
Jock, his five-foot-eight-inch frame drawn up to its
maximum.

The men retreated from the pub, muttering among themselves, piled into three cars and drove off. We spoke to their
intended victim, but he would not commit himself beyond
telling us that the gang were from West London.

The year was 1939 and there was great speculation as to
whether or not there was going to be war. At 11 a.m. on
September 3rd, when the sirens went off all over London,
there were scores of people seeking shelter at Commercial
Street police station. The crowd consisted mainly of Jews
who were refugees from European countries overrun by
the Nazis. They were gradually calmed down and dispersed,
still uneasily expecting the German bombers to come at
any moment.

There was quite a flap in the police hierarchy. 'All police
stations are to be sandbagged immediately,' came the

decree. Volunteers were called for and I joined in. We managed to commandeer two lorries and several policemen were sent to a stockpile of sand, which had been stored in case of emergency. I was with four others building up the sandbags when the first two lorry-loads arrived. Soon the supply of sandbags was greater than we could cope with. I suddenly had an idea.

At the rear of the police station there were a number of lodging houses, full to capacity with Indians. The conditions they lived in were appalling and in some of the buildings they were sleeping on the floor, packed like sardines about twenty to a room. In the past we had had a great deal of trouble from them. A number of white prostitutes who associated with these Indians had been beaten up.

I went round with a uniformed policeman and cleared out the lodging houses until I had a gang of about fifty Indians lined up in the street. There was a great deal of muttering and gesticulating, but I ignored this and marched them up to the station. They were immediately set to work and soon were swarming up the ladders, like ants going up a tree.

In a short time the demand was greater than the supply, so I allocated a dozen to the two lorries and to filling sandbags. Before dark the job was finished and I am certain that ours was the only police station sandbagged in one day. During the operation there were numerous visits by police V.I.P.'s, who were not quite sure whether or not my methods of conscripting labour were orthodox. However, no doubt due to the state of emergency they said nothing.

With the black-out being enforced and every day bringing a fresh threat of bombing, the Police War Reserve was formed. This was popular with a certain cross-section of the public, who had the idea fixed firmly in their minds that being in the War Reserve would exempt them from military service. However, most of the recruits genuinely wanted to do their bit and one of the keenest I met was Joe Loss, the bandleader.

Being small and slightly built, he was the first to admit that he was not exactly a frightening specimen in uniform. He went on patrol as often as he could and when relaxing liked to play solo whist. Many an enjoyable hour I spent in the police canteen playing cards with Joe, pints of beer at our elbows.

Time and again I found the wrestling training received at Peel House a considerable help to me while making arrests requiring some real physical effort.

My instructors had done a good job on me. Originally Stan Bissell had shown me the ropes, but after my selection to represent Scotland as the light heavyweight at the British Empire Games in August 1934, Bert Asserati, the world heavyweight all-in champion, had taken me under his wing. At the Ring, Blackfriars, the heart of world professional wrestling, I wrestled with Bert for hours. It had been as big a disappointment to him as it was to me when the handsome 13 st. 7 lb. Nick Cubbit of South Africa ended my hopes of a medal when he beat me in seven minutes thirty seconds.

The following year, in Edinburgh, in the Scottish Wrestling Championships Bob Marcus, the Scottish light heavyweight champion, put me out of wrestling for some time after I snatched him high in the air in preparation for the dangerous fireman's lift. I felt a tear in the inner wall of my abdomen. The doctors confirmed a hernia with a three-inch tear in the muscular wall.

After my transfer to the C.I.D. I found it virtually impossible to obtain time off to attend wrestling training. My only practice came when the occasional criminal resorted to violence and a wrestler's hold became the most convenient way of pacifying him.

Things were changing at Commercial Street. Jock Black was transferred to the Flying Squad at New Scotland Yard. Two months later I got the surprise of my life when he requested my transfer to join him, and what a difference in routine I found in the hallowed precincts of the Yard.

The Flying Squad consisted of fifty detectives who were

selected from the three thousand C.I.D. officers. The chief inspector in charge was Peter Beveridge, another Border Scot. There was a second-in-command and four detective inspectors, each with a detachment of detectives under his immediate authority.

Flying Squad officers were completely freelance and ranged through every division in the Metropolis. Two detectives were teamed together, usually a sergeant and a constable. These combinations were changed frequently until the pair most suited to each other in a variety of factors, including temperament, were established. Each pair was supplied with a fast car, driver and wireless operator.

For the first spell I was with Jock Black and with him encountered one of the most callous and brutal criminals of my career, Ronald Bertrand Mauri.

A great number of cases of handbag-snatching were reported in an area ranging from Hampstead to Kensington. In most the victims were elderly women. Jock and I decided to haunt the districts concerned and after several days the voice of the wireless operator in the Yard's Information Room told us what we had waited patiently to hear.

'A case of handbag-snatching has been reported in Argyll Gardens, Kensington. The number of the car is YSL 84127. Two men are involved. The car is now heading south-east.'

As we were in the Kensington area and close to the scene we drove to the end of Argyll Gardens. As we did so the wanted car, with two occupants, careered round the corner and drove off towards Kensington High Street. Our driver quickly turned the Squad car around and gave chase. The fleeing car had about two hundred yards of a lead on us and without reducing speed shot into Kensington High Street, across the heavy stream of traffic, miraculously missing a collision, and turned right towards Kensington Road. Fortunately for us, the halted traffic heard the furious ringing of the police car's bell and remained stationary, allowing us a free passage.

The speedometer flickered at 70 m.p.h. as we raced down Kensington Road. We were gradually closing the gap. Our driver saw a clear space on the offside and drove on the wrong side of the lamp-post islands in the centre of the road. Coming in at an angle of thirty degrees we rammed the fugitives' car amidships. There was a great sound of tortured metal and I saw the other driver battling to regain control of his vehicle.

Their car bounced across the pavement, struck a wall and raced away up the street bumping and crashing against the stonework. We closed in once again, but the getaway car slewed round, almost at a right angle, and crossed our path to go up Campden Hill Road. The front nearside wheel was wobbling badly and their speed had dropped to around 40 m.p.h. We accelerated and passed them on the left-hand side, then cut in to block their path. There was another hefty crunch as the two cars collided.

Without wasting a moment they were both out and running along the street. Amazed passers-by shouted, and an old man gallantly tried to force them to stop by swinging his walking stick at them, but he was brushed aside. I chased one man for nearly a hundred yards and when I was close enough threw myself on his back, bringing him crashing to the ground. He fought savagely and with great strength to free himself. He kicked, bit, scratched and punched, and ceased only when, with a vicious wrench, I doubled his right arm and forced it up his back, almost to breaking point. Roland Bertrand Mauri lay at my feet, panting for breath, when Jock Black arrived with the other man, securely handcuffed.

At an identification parade they were both picked out by a number of women who had been attacked and had their handbags stolen. Each time the same formula had been used. Mauri's companion, James Lucas, acted as driver and remained in the car with the engine running while his partner approached the woman and asked directions to a particular street.

When the woman was pointing out the directions Mauri would then strike her a violent blow to the face and snatch the bag. Two women had broken jaws and many of the others had received black eyes and severe bruising, as well as suffering badly from shock.

When the two men were sentenced at the Central Criminal Court, Mauri, who had a number of convictions for violent crimes, received five years' penal servitude, and Lucas, who had been completely under the more ruthless man's domination and had used no violence, was given two years. There were two sequels to Mauri's life after this.

He was serving his term of imprisonment in Dartmoor and when the Italians entered the war on the side of the Nazis, Mauri, who was of Italian extraction, boasted that soon the Italians and Germans would be in England and he would be free once again.

Many of his fellow prisoners, although hardened criminals, were still patriotic. One day when Mauri was released from his cell to go to the exercise yard two prisoners, armed with an earthenware jug and a razor blade, attacked him. A prison officer raced to his aid, but not before Mauri had numerous razor slashes on his face and severe injuries to his eyes, made by the broken mug when it was jabbed in his face.

Later, an emergency operation was made on his right eye, but he was left with severely impaired vision. The two prisoners were sentenced to twenty and eighteen months, to be added to the terms of imprisonment they were already serving.

Because of his injuries Mauri was even more truculent and vicious when he was released. Even previous associates and fellow criminals tried to avoid him.

However, he was not to roam the London streets for long. His days ended on the gallows—hanged for the savage murder of a young girl.

With the German bombing increasing in intensity each night the main duties of the Flying Squad were concentrated on stopping looting. As the West End received a good share of the bombs looting and pilfering was rife. Many arrests were made.

We also spent a good deal of time in the East End, which received heavy punishment from both high explosives and incendiary bombs. On many occasions we returned to the Yard after a night's duty, with the cars damaged by shrapnel from our own anti-aircraft guns. When the barrage was at its height shrapnel fell from the sky like hailstones—large, jagged pieces of metal which ended up buried in the roads, roofs and woodwork. The incendiary bombs, which were phosphorous and weighed about four pounds each, ignited upon impact and were responsible for the majority of the fires.

While working with Detective Sergeant Vic Wynne I found myself on foot in the West End during a remarkably heavy attack.

Bombs and shrapnel were falling fast over a large area and there was a continuous drone from the enemy bombers overhead. When we turned into Dean Street in Soho we decided to pop into the Golden Lion pub for a quick glass of liquid courage. My second whisky had hardly gone down when there was a terrific crash and the bar's customers were showered with glass from the windows and the contents of the counters and shelves. Within seconds incendiaries were bursting all over the place and a large area of Dean Street was ablaze, including St. Mary's Church, directly opposite the pub.

I went upstairs with George Jeffcote, the licensee, to have a look at the damage. We were horrified to find part of the bedroom in flames. Seizing a pair of tongs and wrapping a blanket round my hand, while holding part of it in front of my face, I picked up the incendiary and heaved it out into the street.

We brought the blaze under control and went downstairs. In the reflection of the fires burning outside we saw, for the first time, the devastation in the bar. Many customers

Brodie today, with a salmon fresh from the Dee (*Coopey of Aberdeen*)

1934: British Empire Games wrestler—and constable on the beat in London
Brodie is second right in this group of policemen from various forces who
served with 40 Squadron. Il Duce demands attention

were sitting around, some shocked, and most were bleeding from cuts received from the flying glass.

After George treated us both to a large whisky from a bottle which had been miraculously saved, Vic and I went out into the street to continue our patrol.

There were a number of Canadian soldiers in the middle of the road and a crowd had gathered to watch their antics. Although many of those in the crowd must have been shaken by the bombings and the fires, they were still able to laugh heartily as they watched a young soldier trying to beat out an incendiary with his gas-mask case, which was a mass of flames. He danced around the blazing bomb whooping and shouting. I spotted a second soldier a little further away who seemed also to be engaged in some dervish dance. On closer inspection I found that the heels of his boots were burning, with pieces of flaming phosphorous adhering to them. He was completely tipsy and without thinking had jumped on the burning object to try to extinguish it. I whipped out my pocket knife, cut his laces and pulled off his boots just as the phosphorous burned through to the skin. He was a sorry sight as he limped away, supported by two pals, with his bare, blistered feet.

The fire brigade were now on the scene, but it was many hours before they were able to control the vast number of fires in the area. Poor devils, they looked tired out and weary beyond words, for there had been no let-up for them for weeks on end. These lads bore the brunt of the bombing during London's hours of peril and won the admiration of everyone for their unceasing devotion to duty.

When Vic Wynne was posted to the West End Division I found myself paired off with Sergeant 'Nobby' Clark. On a bright, sunny morning at 9 a.m. as we drove down New Bond Street the wireless informed us of a smash-and-grab raid at Messrs. Hemming and Company, a firm of jewellers in Conduit Street. We did not have far to go and turning a corner saw two cars outside the shop.

One vehicle was on the pavement, drawn hard up against

D

the display window, which had been almost completely shattered. The second car was on the opposite side of the street. A crowd was milling around near the shop window and when I got over to them I saw a man lying on the pavement. A member of the crowd was holding a heavy sledge-hammer, which had been used to smash the window, and was just about to strike the fallen man on the head when I wrenched the weapon from him.

The crowd were obviously disappointed that violence had been averted and one or two gave half-hearted boos. Someone clutched my arm and told me that after the window had been broken two men had rushed over to the car parked opposite. But the driver had been unable to start it and the raiders had bolted. The public-spirited citizens had chased and captured one of them, whom, no doubt, I had saved from severe injury. I dragged him over to the Squad car and left him in the care of the driver and wireless operator.

As I pushed him into the back seat someone shouted: 'Look, guv, up there . . . there's another of them on the roof.'

I glanced upward and saw a man running along a flat roof, five storeys up. I set off in pursuit. When I drew opposite he vanished from sight, but a man, looking out of a second-storey window, gave me a running commentary on his route. Now and again he appeared within my view and when he periodically vanished spectators from other buildings kept me in the picture. I was joined by a uniformed constable whom I told to go well ahead in case the fugitive should find a quick way downstairs.

After crossing the roofs of seven buildings the man finally disappeared from view.

'Keep about four entrances ahead of me,' I shouted to the constable. I waited outside the building where the man had been last seen and it was not long before the constable shouted, waved his arms and ran down some basement steps. I raced to the spot and in the basement saw the constable holding a man whom I recognised instantly as a daring smash-and-grab raider who, though noted for some skilfully executed raids, was never known to use violence. Even if he had wished to be violent on this occasion I doubt very much whether or not he would have been able. He was practically out for the count through sheer physical exhaustion.

When he recovered we marched him to the car where we found the third gang member in custody.

At the Old Bailey several weeks later two of them were each sentenced to three years' penal servitude and the third, who was later to become a powerful West End gang leader, got two years in prison. I have never understood why he got the lighter sentence. When the criminal records of the three were read out, his was easily the worst.

The circumstances surrounding my next meeting with this individual were far more congenial. While on leave from the R.A.F. I found myself drinking in the Premier Club in the West End. I was enjoying a whisky at the bar and in the middle of a chat with Dave Hatter, the proprietor, when he suddenly left me. A few moments later he returned with another whisky.

'You shouldn't have bothered, Dave, I'm sure I owe you far more drinks than you owe me,' I said with a laugh as I took the glass from him.

'Oh, it's not my doing, Allan,' he answered. 'That is from the gentleman standing behind you.'

I looked over my shoulder and there was my former adversary, his face wreathed in smiles.

'How is it going then, guv'nor?' he said, stretching out his hand in welcome.

I shook hands with him and for the next two hours we exchanged stories and drinks, thoroughly enjoying ourselves in the process. The fact that I had been instrumental in sending him to prison for two years did not bother him.

This was typical of the attitude adopted by the true professional criminal of the time, who had been through the hands of the police. Their outlook was, basically, that if they were stupid enough to get caught, then they had no one to blame but themselves. They matched their brains against those of the police. 'May the better man win' could have been their motto.

At long last there appeared an announcement in Police Orders saying that any police officer who wished to volunteer for the Royal Air Force as a pilot or navigator was now free to do so. Wasting no time, I got hold of a typewriter and wrote my formal application. After several attempts—each one being blocked, in one case completely torn up, by my chief, Peter Beveridge—I sought an interview with the Assistant Commissioner in charge of C.I.D., Mr. Ronald Howe, who was knighted in 1955.

A good friend, Lord Waleran, nephew of Lord Glentanar my former employer, had told me before he set out for service in the Air Force that if I ever needed help from the top of the police tree I should contact Mr. Howe, who was a good friend of his. As I desperately wanted to have a go in the R.A.F. and was becoming frustrated by the blocking of my applications, I marched straight in and confronted the Assistant Commissioner, using the pretence that 'I have a personal message from a Lord Waleran' to grant me entrance to the hallowed corridors of power. He gave me a sympathetic hearing and placed his signature of approval on the application form.

Two months later, on August 13, 1941, as aircrew cadet Brodie I entered another world.

With my eyes fixed on gaining a pilot's wings I studied mathematics, elementary air navigation, aircraft recognition, Morse code and a variety of other seconds. After two months the theory was over and I passed out from the course with a good mark behind me. Eighteen days later I set off from Greenock aboard the 33,000-ton *Louis Pasteur*, for practical flying training in the United States.

Eleven days later we docked at Halifax, Nova Scotia, and in various stages travelled by train across Canada and through America to arrive at Maxwell Field Air Force Base, near Montgomery, Alabama. We lived in this camp for four weeks and during our stay the Japanese bombed Pearl Harbour. America was well and truly in the war.

Our course was split up and sent to various training fields. With nineteen others I went to Arcadia, Florida, on the edge of the Everglade Swamps. Wasting no time our instructors put us straight on to Steerman aircraft (the equivalent of the British Tiger Moth) and after seven and a half hours of dual flying with an excellent tutor I was sent aloft on my first solo flight.

I found the take-off relatively easy, but at three thousand feet I wondered if I would be able to land safely. The truth was that I did not feel like coming down anyway—the sheer exhilarating thrill of flight had won me over completely. The thrill of piloting a light aircraft must surely be one of life's greatest physical sensations.

Trying to remember all I had been taught, I eventually started to lose height and when the aircraft was on the approach leg, cut the engine and glided in at around 90 m.p.h. Twenty feet off the ground I levelled off and held the aircraft down until the wheels touched down in a three-point landing. I still maintain that my first solo landing was one of the best I ever did.

After sixty hours' flying we moved to Macon, in Georgia, for the second and more complicated phase of training. We were now flying Vultees, heavy brutes of aircraft, and had to get used to landing under power, as against the glide landings of the Steerman. We went through dual-flying training before going solo and carried out cross-country flights, night trips and instrument flying. My logbook showed sixty hours on Vultees when disaster struck.

As I was down on the flying roster for a cross-country flight the next afternoon I decided to let my hair down. With some kindly people who lived near the base I went on the town and wined and dined beyond the bounds of normality. It was 4 am. when I crawled back into bed.

At 8 a.m. I forced myself in the direction of the hangar to report for duty. My head was thick, my tongue furred and I looked forward to sitting back to enjoy endless cups of hot steaming coffee destined to put fresh life into me. As I signed the duty book I glanced at the roster to see which one of my pals was going up for the first period of solo flying. To my horror I saw a name crossed out and in block capitals mine had been inserted above. There was absolutely nothing I could do but go.

Feeling drowsy and heavy, I got out my parachute, noted the number of the aircraft assigned to me, and signed out. With a casual look around I climbed into the cockpit, started the engine and let it run for several minutes to warm up. Without properly checking all the controls and instruments, I taxied to the end of the runway and started to take off.

I gradually eased the throttle open and at first the Vultee behaved normally as she raced down the runway. As she gained speed I felt a great pressure on the rudder control and joystick, but thought nothing of it as the aircraft lifted off the ground. Almost as soon as the wheels broke contact I found myself using all my strength on the joystick in an effort to keep the aircraft level. I snatched one hand away from the stick and attempted to turn the aileron control. This was my undoing. When the full pressure on the stick was eased off the aircraft went into a spin and plummeted towards the ground from a height of about seventy feet. The sound of the crash was almost deafening and the Vultee fell over on to her back. Fortunately the tailplane remained intact and held part of the twisted fuselage off the ground while I climbed through the shattered canopy— my only injuries a few bruises.

As I stood up I remembered the all-important Form 1A which was carried in the aircraft and filled in by every pilot prior to take-off. I had not signed it. I crawled back under the Vultee and was groping around in the cockpit in a frantic effort to find the form before one of the flying instructors arrived on the scene, when I heard a vehicle drive up. A few seconds later a voice remarked: 'Poor blighter—he's had it.'

Without laying my hands on the elusive form I crawled out once more to confront my prophets of doom. The two ambulance men looked quite shocked when they spotted their corpse slithering out from under the fuselage. They were even more amazed when I said there was nothing wrong with me.

There were several interviews with officers and other interrogations before the day of the Crash Board. Standing before a table and confronted by three colonels I admitted not checking the controls prior to take-off. I was dismissed from the course for my negligence. The three colonels were quite humane—they informed me that I was still free to continue my flying training but that I would have to start from scratch.

I was sent to Ponca City, Oklahoma, in the heart of the oil country, but after twelve hours, again on Vultees, the instructor informed me that he was recommending that I begin all over again. This was probably for my own good, but the thought of going over all the old familiar ground once more was too much for me. I asked for a transfer to Canada and to re-muster as a bomb-aimer.

My request was granted and at the bombing and gunnery schools at Paulson, Manitoba, and in Regina, Saskatchewan, began the happiest spell of my Air Force training. The operation of bomb-sights and machine guns seemed to come naturally to me and soon I was proficient in the handling of both. I had now found my true niche in the Royal Air Force.

5

The Desert Moon My Witness

WHEN the course was over I was commissioned and
given the thin blue bands of a pilot officer to wear on my
epaulettes. Aboard the *Queen Mary* I returned to Britain and
after fourteen days' leave arrived, in my brand-new officer's
uniform, at Moreton-in-Marsh, Gloucestershire, for the
training which would equip me for operational flying.
Scores of aircrew were waiting to be teamed up and rumour
was rife that we were all destined for the Middle East. In
the lecture hall the Commanding Officer told us that we
would be given forty-eight hours to sort ourselves out
and pick our own crews.

Most made for the mess bar—sergeants, flight-sergeants
and officers alike. No distinction was made between officers
and non-commissioned ranks at this stage.

An Australian officer with pilot's wings caught my eye
and as I liked the look of him I introduced myself and
bought a couple of drinks. He said his name was Reg
Dolden. We were soon in agreement to team up and decided
to work together to pick the three remaining members of
our crew.

Next morning at breakfast I sat next to a big Irish rear
gunner. He seemed a steady, reliable type, so I gave Reg
a nudge and nodded towards the Irishman. After our meal
the three of us had a chat together and Mike Irwin decided
to join us. He said he knew of two Australian sergeants who
might be willing to join as well. They were inseparable

companions—a navigator and wireless operator. They were exactly the types we wanted and when approached agreed immediately to fly with us.

We were indeed a mixed bunch. Our pilot, Reg Dolden (27), had previously worked in his father's wheat-and-chaff business in Cormullah, Sydney; Mike Irwin (29), the Irish rear gunner, had been employed in an insurance office in Edinburgh; Kevin Connolly (23), the navigator, was tall and powerfully built and burned a deep brown from outdoor work in Australia; Bobby Bramhall (24), our wireless operator, also from Australia, was slim and good-looking; and myself, now aged twenty-nine. We had a high average age in comparison with most crews. Fifty per cent of the lads in the pool were under twenty-one—indeed many of them had come straight into the Air Force from school.

As we drew our flying kits we counted ourselves fortunate that we had been able to come to a mutual agreement to team up. Those unable to make up their own minds were formed into crews by the Commanding Officer. In many cases the results were disastrous. There was often a complete lack of confidence in each other; in some cases men who disliked each other found themselves forced into flying together. In a life where harmony amongst crew members was the ticket to staying alive, obviously this situation could lead to no good.

Our aircraft were Wellingtons, rather elderly specimens, and the pilots were the first to go up, flying for about eight hours as second pilots before taking over themselves. When their flying was deemed satisfactory full crew training began. Reg was a most methodical pilot and insisted that I should stand beside his seat to ensure that all the cockpit drill was carried out and to watch the instruments on take-off and landing.

As time passed we progressed from day to night flying and infra-red 'bombing'. This entailed precision navigation, as the target was usually a remote village where an infra-red light was displayed. Instead of bombs a camera was carried and when the bomb switch was pressed the camera was set in motion.

When the film was developed it was soon discovered whether or not we had been successful in scoring a 'hit' on our target. During these flights my job was to map read. I was not allowed to interfere with the course given by the navigator to the pilot until the estimated time of arrival on target (E.T.A.). Only then could I direct the pilot on his course. We discovered soon enough that we had nothing to fear from our navigation, as Kev proved thoroughly reliable, although he liked plenty of time to concentrate on plotting the course.

Balloon barrages were always a constant source of worry on our cross-country flights. Although we were usually routed clear of them, we had several nasty moments when the winds changed and we were blown off course.

With one operation completed—an uneventful leaflet-dropping raid on Nantes—our posting came through: to Burma. Several other crews were also posted to the Far East while the remainder were bound for North Africa.

Next day we were briefed on our route and issued with the remainder of our kit. Each man was given a .38 Smith and Wesson revolver and ammunition, a pocket compass, escape kit, silk maps and binoculars (night and day). Last, but far from least, we became the proud recipients of a brand-new Wellington Mk. 10. What a contrast it was to the battered and much-used bomber we had trained in, with its old, and usually unserviceable, equipment. Our new prize was able to carry a full bomb load while maintaining a cruising speed of around 180 m.p.h. When empty we could push her up to 210 m.p.h.

The air tests on our new Wellington completed, we set off on March 14, 1943, on the first leg of our long haul to Burma. The first stage was a short one and we landed to refuel at Port Reath, on the most southerly coast of Cornwall. It was a wild yet beautiful spot, with the landing strip terminating at the very edge of sheer, rugged cliffs. After a meal and with a full fuel load on board we taxied out to prepare for take-off. A Beaufort was given clearance to get airborne immediately in front. I watched it start its run down towards the sea. As it flashed past the half-way mark it lifted off the ground for a few feet, then settled back on the tarmac once more.

Reg shouted: 'Good God, he'd better get his bloody wheels up soon or there's going to be trouble!'

I felt sick as I watched the Beaufort streak away, still on the ground, struggling like some wounded bird to rise into the sky.

With mixed feelings of horror and frustration, because we were powerless to help, we saw the aircraft reach the runway's end. The huge tail reared up into the sky, hung suspended in mid-air for a fraction of a second, then was gone from view as the bomber and occupants plunged headlong for hundreds of feet into the sea that boiled around and spewed over the reefs at the cliff-base.

Reg did not give us time to brood over the tragedy. He immediately requested permission to take off and, when this was granted, put the Wellington under power. We had all been shaken by the disaster and the seconds that ticked by until we felt our trusty machine lift off were tense and nerve-racking. There was no sign of the Beaufort in the sea below—only the white-flecked crest of the surf.

It took six hours twenty-five minutes to reach Gibraltar, where we stayed for four days while the engines were thoroughly overhauled—the last major service they were to receive for some time. On March 19 we set off across Algeria, south of Tunisia, then north-east over the Sahara Desert, to Castel Benito, in Tripolitania.

Our first greeting came from a small man dressed in a dirty pair of shorts and equally filthy bush jacket and sporting about three days' growth of beard. His face was haggard and drawn and he introduced himself as Wing Commander Holmes, Commanding Officer of Number 40 Squadron.

He said bluntly: 'You can forget all about Burma. Oh yes. You are staying here. I want both aircraft and crew to go on ops tonight.'

Both Reg and I protested vigorously, despite the difference in rank.

'You can't do that, sir,' Reg told him. 'We've been given our orders—surely they can't be changed now.'

The Wing Commander took our rebellious attitude in good part, despite his tiredness.

'You are jolly well staying here, whether you like it or not. As for your previous orders—forget them. I'm sending an immediate signal informing headquarters that you will be operating from here—as from now.'

We submitted gracefully, saluted, and went back to our aircraft to inform the others of the change in plans. Our freight, bound for India, was unloaded and we were told to get some food and sleep before reporting for briefing, prior to the bombing mission. It was to be the Wing Commander's last operation of his tour. He was to fly the aircraft and Reg would be second pilot.

In a dilapidated wooden building in a corner of the camp we found three crews resting on their camp-beds. They had been bombing the previous night and had completed a double raid on German troops and transport near Sfax. The Number 40 Squadron base was twenty-six miles south of Misurata at El Gardabia in the Sahara Desert, about one hundred miles east of Tripoli. When on double raids they refuelled and bombed-up again at Castel Benito. The previous night's raid had been particularly tiring, so Wing Commander Holmes and the rest of his crews had stayed over for a rest before returning to El Gardabia.

That night as I lay in the bomb-aimer's compartment as we neared our target—the main coast road at Sfax—I experienced the true meaning of the word adventure. A sense of excitement had often come to me before, in the face of danger as a policeman, but it had never matched the thrill I felt as I listened to the throbbing of the two powerful engines and felt the fuselage vibrate as it was buffeted by pockets of turbulence. As I lined up the Mark IV bomb-sight and fingered the release button it was difficult to control the pounding in my head, the fierce beating of my heart.

'Heading for target; over to you, bomb-aimer.'

The Wing Commander's voice jerked me back to reality. I opened the bomb doors, looked along the parallel wires of the bomb-sight and started to give directions for holding course.

These were brief and to the point. A 'right' or 'left' followed by 'steady' when the aircraft moved slightly off course.

After several corrections the target showed straight along the centre of the sighting wires. I saw the intersecting cross-wire meet the road. This was it. Quickly I pressed the button and released the full bomb load.

As the 250 lb. general-purpose bombs dropped away, a furious barrage of shells burst around us. The Wellington heaved violently and lurched over on her starboard wing. A pungent smell of cordite enveloped me.

I climbed up into the front turret and swivelled it round. I saw that the upper edge of the starboard wing was riddled with holes and the fabric covering the framework was in ribbons.

As I searched for more damage the sticks of bombs exploded across the road. At the same time a photo flash went off at about one thousand feet.

Every night bomber was fitted with a large F.24 camera, automatically operated by the pressure of the bomb button. The photo flash was dropped with the bombs and a vivid picture obtained of the target with the 1,000,000 candle-power explosion of light.

As I realised we had struck home I let out a Red Indian-like whoop of joy and the rest of the crew joined in from their various positions in the aircraft.

The situation was ripe for a fire and for the first stage of our return journey we watched like hawks for the tell-tale signs of a flame. An inspection of the fuselage revealed dozens of shrapnel holes, but fortunately no vital part seemed to have been hit.

As we flew back we saw flashes of artillery fire far below us. The Eighth Army and Rommel's troops were locked in combat.

No fire materialised and we landed safely on the rough runway, marked on either side by lines of paraffin flares.

Next morning when we went to look at our Wellington we discovered that Lady Luck had indeed been kind to us. There were twenty large holes in the fuselage and starboard wing, plus hundreds of smaller ones where shrapnel had cut through. Several hits had been scored around the edge of the wing fuel tank. A few inches to the left and the tank would almost certainly have exploded.

We settled down to a steady programme of bombing landing strips, roads, railway lines, troop concentrations, transport and ammunition dumps, usually flying with a minimum petrol load and maximum quantity of bombs. The bombs now varied from 250 lb. and 500 lb. general purpose to 40 lb. anti-personnel. The former were used with short delay fuses for cratering the roads and railways and blowing up buildings and bridges, while the latter burst on impact, spraying the surrounding area with vicious fragments of shrapnel.

There were very few raids carried out without the Wellington returning unscathed, but on April 12 we all thought that our luck had run out for good.

We were ordered to bomb a landing strip at Menzel Temime, far into Tunisia, where there was a concentration of German fighters. This was one of the last serviceable airfields left to the enemy and was heavily defended. We were warned to expect trouble from night fighters— Ju. 88s.

We took off at 6.55 p.m. as darkness fell. The first part of the journey was smooth until we crossed back over the coast and met with spasmodic patches of light flak. German radar operators had now grown extremely proficient and we were forced to fly a zigzag course with me map-reading for most of the trip inland.

Bobby stood beside Reg in the cockpit, keeping a sharp look-out for the first sign of the enemy fighters. Mike did likewise in the rear turret. Poor Kev was stuck in the tiny navigator's cabin, hard at work on plotting the course, and apart from the conversation on the intercom knew little of what was going on outside his own little world.

At last in the sharp, clear light of the moon I could see our target lying ahead of us. Apart from the drone of the engines there was an ominous air of quietness inside the aircraft. It was usually like this when a crew approached their target. No matter how brave one appeared on the outside, that hidden, lurking prick of fear always lay dormant, waiting for release. Bobby was now in the front gun turret and Kev took over beside the pilot's seat. We were at six thousand feet and felt naked and vulnerable in the bright light of the desert moon. Reg altered course and flew straight and level on the bombing run.

I watched the target coming up nicely along the grid wires of the bomb-sight and got ready for the release. Then all hell broke loose. A master searchlight caught us in its beam and was followed quickly by several others. Simultaneously a heavy barrage of light and heavy guns opened up. Despite the buffeting from the heavy shells bursting around us Reg managed to hold the Wellington on course.

There was an ear-splitting crash and a blinding flash just under my window and I felt a violent blow on the head. I was almost stunned and reached up to hold my aching head. My hands felt wet and sticky and I saw the blood. There was a steady stream pouring down my face and neck.

The aircraft lurched round as if in a drunken stupor and my bomb-sight was a mangled, ugly piece of metal. It was utterly useless.

Through my head-set I could hear Reg calling. His voice seemed dim and faint and I wondered if my eardrums had been damaged by the heavy blast.

'Are you all right down there?' he queried.

I managed to reply: 'Yes, fine. Can you hold her for about thirty seconds?'

'Yes, I think so—anyway, I'll have a damned good try. Sure you can manage?'

'Sure thing. Just hold her steady.'

'Roger.'

We began to lose height and by trial and error I estimated we had reached our correct bombing position. I released the stick of bombs and as they hurtled earthwards the ground gunners opened up with everything they had.

The Wellington bucked and heaved and the fuselage lashed around like some giant fish trying to escape from the hook that holds it fast. Black smoke and giant sheets of flame leaped skywards as our bombs found their mark through the parked aircraft. A fuel-storage tank disintegrated in a thousand pieces—its contents a fierce, fiery furnace.

Now that our bombs had done their work, my job was over in the tiny cubicle. I climbed up to join Reg.

To my amazement I found him partially slumped over the controls and Kev was battling to hold the control column back and shift the pilot's weight away from it. I took over and eased Reg back into his seat.

I turned to help Kev and it took plenty of effort from both of us to get the Wellington back under control again.

Kev told me that when the aircraft was hit Reg had been thrown forward by the terrific force and had crashed into the control column. His right arm and shoulder were out of action but did not seem to be broken. Kev, too, had been thrown forward and received a bad shaking. I called up Mike in the rear and Bobby in the front turret and they both replied that they were uninjured—although they had

Fort Dixon, a police outpost deep in the jungle of Pahang
A helicopter brings in supplies to Fort Dixon

The funeral of a police lieutenant, killed by terrorists in Selangor. The stones mark the graves of other victims

With a jungle detachment of police at a field post in Kedah

been knocked about quite a bit. I could tell by their voices that they, too, had been shaken badly. My head still continued to bleed but the pain had gone. The blood, running into my eyes and under my collar, was more of a nuisance than anything else. Kev had a look at my injuries and confirmed several large gashes.

'You're bloody lucky to have a head at all, you jammy Scotsman,' he laughed, as he gave my shoulder a playful cuff. I felt much better after hearing his sense of humour returning.

Reg had perked up a bit, but refused to leave the pilot's seat. With his left hand gripping the control column he attempted to hold the bomber steady. We were still under a considerable bombardment and I helped him with the controls as we dived to two hundred feet in an attempt to dodge the searchlights and flak.

The Wellington was now ungainly and heavy to handle and it grew bitterly cold as a chill wind raced through the gaping void in the belly.

When we cleared the last of the anti-aircraft guns and were out over the sea Kev helped Reg out of the pilot's seat and I took over the controls. With the thrill of flying an aircraft once more I almost completely forgot the likelihood of there being German fighters in the vicinity. But Kev and Bobby kept their eyes open and apart from a couple of false alarms we made it back unscathed.

Reg insisted that he be in his seat to take the Wellington in to land. I was a bit apprehensive about this, as he seemed to be in great pain. Every so often I could see him clench his fists and grit his teeth as a spasm of pain passed through him. We let him have his way and he agreed that I could help him with the landing. Bobby informed Flying Control that we might have trouble getting down, as our undercarriage light had not come on when the switch to lower the wheels was selected. Kev had a look, but although the wheels appeared to be down in position he could not be sure whether or not they had locked.

E

Three hundred feet . . . two hundred feet . . . one hundred feet. Reg was almost crying out with the pain as he was forced to put weight on the controls and the rudders. I followed his every move and took as much weight as possible in shifting the controls.

The flares stretched away into the distance and the Wellington's nose was continually caught in cross-winds forcing us away from the centre line. At fifty feet she tried once more to break free from our control and the nose swung upwards.

The air-speed indicator wobbled hesitantly and for an instant the bomber was close to stalling. I increased the power and the Wellington steadied up. Reg and I forced her down.

Off centre, but still on the strip, we bumped down to earth. All we could do was hang on and hope for the best as the bomber raced along the runway trying hard to crab to the port side. Reg had all but passed out by the time we slithered to a halt, about three-quarters of the way along the runway and almost on top of the paraffin flares. The fire tenders raced up with an ambulance right behind them and in fifteen minutes we were having our wounds attended to in the field hospital at Group Headquarters.

Reg had a severely strained shoulder and extensive bruising, which required considerable strapping, while I had my head wounds cleaned and stitched. The biggest, right on top of my head, had almost scalped me and the orderly attending to me kept on repeating that I had lost a great deal of blood. I assured him on an equal number of occasions that I could see this for myself, judging by the state of my flying suit.

The old Wellington was a sorry sight too. The engines were untouched but the fabric on the fuselage hung in tatters. The bomb-aimer's panel had vanished completely leaving a large ragged hole.

All that remained of the bomb-sight were several pieces of scrap metal where it had taken the full force of a large chunk of shrapnel. There was no doubt that it had saved my life.

We now had a new commanding officer—Wing Commander Douglas Bagnall, D.F.C., a New Zealander, and Reg, Mike and myself were all promoted. We were all made flight-lieutenants and took over new responsibilities as flight commander, gunnery leader and bombing leader, respectively.

Under Douglas Bagnall a new pattern of operations was worked out. Bombing was now done as one complete operation, involving several aircraft all dropping their loads at two-minute intervals. Many of the squadron's aircraft were in pretty poor shape and it was only due to the industry, care and attention lavished on them by their efficient ground crews that many of them were able to stagger off the runway with a full load of bombs. No praise could be high enough for these backroom boys, who got all the dirty work to do and very little recognition for their efforts.

Each crew looked after their particular aircraft with the care of a doting mother. Not only did they keep the aircraft up to scratch but they always had some word of encouragement for the crew. One of the saddest sights on a bomber squadron was to see the ground crews of missing aircraft waiting for their charges to return. They would hang around the airfield for long enough, always hoping that their particular machine might be limping back on one engine and that, miraculously, it would soon appear overhead. When all hope was gone they would sadly return to their quarters and an air of gloom would descend on the engineering section for days afterwards.

The Germans were now being pushed back into the Cape Bon tip of Tunisia—their position made even more precarious by the threat of the First Army advancing from Algeria. Night after night we bombed and strafed the beaches and soon the North African phase of the war was over.

The squadron moved to Kharouan and I found it a pleasant change to have pomegranate orchards, stretching for miles on either side of the camp, instead of a dry, burning inferno of sand.

We landed at Tripoli on one occasion, after a raid, and as I entered the mess a small white terrier came crawling towards me. He had large, round pleading eyes and was thin and emaciated. When I picked him up he whined and licked my hands as if saying, 'Thanks, mate.' No one else in the mess claimed him, so after feeding him up I took him back to base. He was pure white, with black eyes and nose, and during the flight to Kharouan sat on my knee completely unperturbed by the roar of the engines.

Because his lower jaw protruded slightly I decided to christen him Il Duce—after the Italian dictator. He was not long in settling into his new surroundings and became my shadow, never leaving my side in case he should lose me. Il Duce became our mascot and flew with me on more than thirty bombing missions.

We all felt unhappy for days, after we lost him in a small village in the Apennine Mountains. While returning from two weeks' leave we stopped to have a meal in the mountain village. Il Duce got out of the truck, lifted his head high, gave a loud whine and raced away up the street as if all the demons in hell were pursuing him. That was the last I saw of him, although we combed the village from end to end.

My heart was heavy when we finally drove away—my only consolation being that the bitch he found on the lovely mountainside might be faithful to him.

Reg and I laid claim to the first Wellington, sent to the Middle East, specially adapted to carry a 4,000 lb. blockbuster. Blockbusters were evil-looking weapons of war, shaped like a huge metal barrel, covered with a wafer-thin casing and packed with high explosives.

We dropped the first one on the railway sidings at Palermo and I was staggered by the devastating force of destruction we had unleashed. Complete railway engines and trucks were thrown bodily into the air and as we banked away from the target area a mass of flame spread out beneath us.

When Sicily was invaded on the night of July 10, 1943, we were all given individual targets. Ours was the seaplane base at Syracuse. Loaded with nine 500 lb. bombs, armed with five-second delay fuses, we headed across the Mediterranean towards the south-east coast of Sicily. We could see the invasion fleet ploughing through the sea and, although we could hear nothing because of the complete radio silence, we knew that hundreds of aircraft were in the sky that night.

At one hundred feet we flew over a collection of wireless masts, and as we cleared the hangars at the water's edge, I released the bombs. Reg opened up the throttles and we climbed steeply to clear the town. From the rear turret Mike told us that the bombs had done their work—several of the hangars were on fire.

We climbed to six thousand feet and watched the first of the American Dakotas arrive on the scene. The ones nearest to us were carrying parachutists and what happened in the next few minutes was the most cruel waste of human life I have ever witnessed.

To our horror, we saw the parachutists start to jump while they were more than five miles off-shore, then in varying distances towards the land. A few were lucky and hit the shore, but for many their leap into space was a leap into death. Those who were dropped far out to sea did not have any hope of survival—they were dragged under and drowned, unable to move with the vast canopy of silk turning into a leaden weight when it hit the water.

I have never been able to understand what the American pilots were thinking about in allowing these men to be dropped at this position. The dropping zone could be seen clearly from a long way off. I can only think that for many of the pilots it was their first operational trip and that they panicked when they saw the light flak coming from the shore batteries. Further south the gliders and parachutists towed and carried by British aircraft landed smack on target and met with only a mediocre resistance.

Back at base the topic of conversation for days afterwards was of the unfortunate men who had been dropped needlessly to a watery grave. I only hope that the American crews of the Dakotas responsible for this appalling tragedy never met up with the Parachute Regiment again.

From the date of the invasion we were bombing, nightly, the ports of Messina and Palermo as well as the Italian mainland ports as far north as Naples.

One day during this period, when we were on standdown for twenty-four hours, Reg and I were called from the mess bar and told that the Commanding Officer wished to see us. When we entered his office Douglas Bagnall greeted us heartily and handed us a wireless form bearing a message he had just received from the U.K. It said simply that we had both been awarded the Distinguished Flying Cross.

The Wing Commander expressed his congratulations and said that the recommendation had been made shortly after the night Reg had been injured during the raid on Menzel Temime. The handshaking over, we headed for the mess, where, in no time, we had quite a party going—a ration of whisky was issued and a quantity of beer unearthed and rapidly demolished.

The destruction of Recco Viaduct, east-south-east of Genoa, was to be our next problem. This viaduct spanned a deep cleft in the rocky coast and carried a double set of railway tracks between a tunnel at either side. It was completely flanked by towering cliffs at both ends and to the landward side. Judging by the reconnaissance photographs, it appeared that the cleft in the rocks extended inland for about one hundred yards beyond the viaduct and was about one hundred and fifty yards wide. The Americans had already dropped hundreds of bombs from a high level but had completely missed the target. It appeared to be impregnable.

I suggested that one 4,000 lb. blockbuster, fitted with an eleven-second delay fuse, dropped from a low altitude, might do the trick. Wing Commander Bagnall was interested and after a discussion agreed that the project had a reasonable chance of success.

Before the operation we concentrated on low-level bombing and for several days dropped smoke bombs from a height of fifty feet, while banking the Wellington at an angle of forty-five to fifty degrees, over a partly submerged wreck in the sea near Cape Monastir.

At 3 p.m. on November 10 we took off with our big bomb nestling in the Wellington's belly and two flare-dropping aircraft accompanying us. Their job was to illuminate the viaduct as we made our bombing run. Because of the heavy bomb we were unable to carry sufficient fuel to allow us to make the flight in one hop. At Decimomannu, in southern Sardinia, we touched down to fill up our tanks and at 7.40 p.m. headed north over Sardinia and Corsica.

At four thousand five hundred feet I was able to obtain a clear view of the viaduct, standing grim and grey, its stonework bathed in the moon's cold light. Wing Commander Bagnall dropped the Wellington down to one hundred feet as we swept in over the sea. The first flare-dropping aircraft released a stick of flares but without much effect—only one illuminated.

The bomb-aimer's panel looked bare without the bomb-sight, which had been removed because it could not be used at such a low level and at the steep angle required for bombing.

We made five dummy runs, each one bringing us closer to the viaduct. The cliffs reared up above us and to the north I could see the buildings on the outskirts of the town of Recco. On the sixth run a stick of flares exploded, providing us with perfect light, but I could see we would have to get even closer in order to be successful.

I switched on the intercom and called up the pilot.

'I think we should try to go around again—we're only about twenty to thirty yards away from the release point. Can you manage it?'

The Wing Commander assured me that he could.

'Hang on to your hat down there, old fellow. I'll bring her round, and in again, just for you. Mind you, we'll be at a hell of a steep angle and don't be too surprised if you hear the wing-tips scraping those bloody cliffs as we go by.'

He switched off the intercom and I felt the Wellington go into a steep bank. Round we went in the tightest turn I have ever experienced. The Wellington behaved perfectly as we came round, almost standing on a wing-tip.

I saw the viaduct flash by beneath me. It was now or never.

The aircraft was practically catapulted upwards as she gave birth to her giant bomb. The pilot increased the power as we climbed away. Every ounce of speed was necessary, as we only had eleven seconds to get clear of the area before the blast.

Mike gave us the news from his eyrie in the rear.

'She's exploded bang on—and what a fire,' came his excited voice.

We circled back and saw that a huge section of the viaduct had been completely destroyed and that a train emerging from the tunnel on the north side had been caught up by the blast. The engine and the first three coaches were burning fiercely, while all along the track the remaining coaches were scattered about, some on their sides, while others were in heaps, standing on end. Judging by the number of people milling around, it appeared to be a troop train.

When reconnaissance photographs were taken two days later the wreckage of the train had been removed but the mammoth gap in the viaduct remained untouched. It was established that a number of the viaduct's main supports had been destroyed as well. The disruption of this main line, carrying reinforcements of troops and supplies, was a major blow to the Nazis and we had managed to accomplish it without a single shot being fired at us.

6

Always Look Before You Leap

One of the most foolhardy remarks I have ever made—
at least it seemed that way immediately after I uttered it
—was, 'Any bloody fool can jump out of an aeroplane.'

Unfortunately the man I addressed it to was Captain
Temple, the Officer Commanding the Allied Parachutist
School, at San Vico, near Brindisi, in Italy.

I was now stationed at Brindisi with the Balkan Air
Transport Service, flying weapons, ammunition, food and
medical supplies into Yugoslavia to aid the Partisans,
locked in their bitter struggle with the Germans. On our
return journeys we brought out the wounded.

I made the remark during a party in the mess where a
considerable number of strangers, mostly army officers,
were present. Next day Captain Temple played his own
little joke on me by telling my Commanding Officer,
Group Captain Underhill, that I had volunteered for a
parachutist course. I had no option but to accept the
challenge and two days later found myself on one of the
most rushed parachutist courses in the business. Ten of the
twelve pupils were Italian patriots, from northern Italy,
who were due to be dropped in that area in five days' time.

We started at dawn and for the first day were subjected
to a dozen ingenious methods of torture, culminating in
what must have been the Commanding Officer's trump
card—a ride down a steel hawser. This consisted of a stout
cable, strung tightly from the top of a twenty-foot platform,

running down to a height of six feet above the ground and secured at this end to a large tree-trunk. The distance between the two points was only fifteen yards, making the angle of descent extremely acute. A deep sandpit had been dug beneath the contraption.

We stood around, viewing the entire set-up with great apprehension—no man wished to be first to test it out.

'Right then, Brodie, I think you should have a go. Remember any bloody fool can jump out of . . .'

I did not give Captain Temple a chance to say any more.

'Right, sir, I don't mind,' I shouted, and climbed up to the lofty platform. I grasped the two leather loops, fitted to the hawser, and the sergeant, standing on the ground near the spot where my drop from the pulley should start, gave me the go-ahead.

Trying to remember all I had been taught about rolling, I launched myself into space and relinquished my hold on the hawser when opposite the sergeant. By this time I had gained quite a forward impetus and when landing forgot to bend my knees and turn my shoulder inwards in preparation for the textbook roll. The sand felt like concrete when I hit it and for several moments I thought my neck and back must be broken. My whole body ached when I picked myself up, but within an hour I was aloft once more, this time swinging down to a more orthodox landing.

There was no relaxation from the training—four hours after our lesson on the contraption, as I prefer to call it, we were six hundred feet up in the air, our parachutes strapped to our backs, ready to jump from a Dakota in pitch darkness. Again Captain Temple reserved the dubious honour of going first especially for me.

The despatcher gave me the signal to get ready. I secured the release strap to the rings on my parachute and moved forward to the exit door. The first prickle of apprehension ran over me as I remembered I was six hundred feet above the ground, about to throw myself into nothingness.

I had just started to regret my stupid remark about fools

when the green light flashed on. Before I knew what I was doing I felt myself falling, with my head back, chin in and feet together. A sharp tug told me that my parachute had opened and I felt my rate of descent slow down.

I reached up to pull down on the parachute straps, with the intention of releasing them about twenty feet from the ground, to cushion my drop, when I hit the earth with a sickening thud. I had no time to roll over, instead I was pitched forward, all the wind knocked from my body. A gentle breeze was blowing and seconds later the canopy began to settle gently on top of me. I lay like this for almost five minutes as the remainder of my companions from the Dakota dropped down and landed in a wide area around me.

When I got back to the training school Captain Temple was on hand to greet me. He could hardly wait to ask whether or not I had experienced a fairly heavy landing. I assured him that I most certainly had.

'Sorry about that, old chap,' he said, with a grin on his face, 'you got the wrong 'chute. Yours was a twenty-eight-foot 'chute instead of a thirty-two-foot one, which, as you know, is the correct size for a man of your weight!'

I completed seven more jumps, from heights varying from four hundred feet to eight hundred feet, during the next two days and almost as quickly as it had started I found the course at an end. I was a fully qualified parachutist.

Back at Brindisi, Group Captain Underhill had problems —the theft of parachutes from operational aircraft and several acts of sabotage.

The aerodrome and repair workshops were under the guard of five hundred Italian civil and military policemen, but the Group Captain was not satisfied with them. He wanted me to take on the job of security officer, because of my previous police experience, and he offered me a completely free hand to use what methods I felt were necessary to curb the present wave of trouble.

One day later, after surveying my new command, I was back in his office demanding the sacking of the five hundred

Italians. The Group Captain was completely taken aback and argued for ten minutes, protesting that I was urging an extremely serious step.

I heard the phrase 'It could have dangerous consequences' repeated on numerous occasions during the discussion. At last he agreed, admitting that it was possible that the Italians were responsible. He also agreed that the two hundred Yugoslavs, who had been discharged from hospital and were recuperating in a nearby camp, before returning to fight, could take the Italians' place.

The Italian police commandant, a colonel, was a charming man. I told him that I wanted his men withdrawn as I suspected their inefficiency and in some cases their dishonesty had been the cause of much trouble.

'I hope,' I said, as forcefully as I could, 'that you will raise no objections.'

He waved his hands flamboyantly and leaned back in a magnificent armchair.

'But no, I will have no objections to make. Get rid of them if you wish. I will be only too happy to co-operate,' he assured me.

He bent forward as if to impart a confidence.

'You see these men—these policemen—they are all from the south.'

He tapped his chest with two slim fingers.

'I, Mr. Brodie, am from the north. In the north, good and honourable people—in the south, well, there are a lot of rogues among them.'

Next day the change-over took place. I had no difficulty in obtaining the services of the Yugoslavs, as I was the liaison officer at their camp. Knowing their hatred for the Italians, I warned them not to use any violence except in the line of self-defence or the protection of property. I drew thirty rifles and bayonets and ten Sten guns from the armoury and for each tour of duty issued ten rounds to each rifle-holder and two full magazines for each Sten.

I set up an orderly room inside the camp which was completely surrounded by a six-foot barbed-wire fence and patrolled night and day by the guards. No one was allowed to enter without a permit, issued by myself. Notices were displayed all over the place stating that no Italian would be allowed near the aircraft, stores or other buildings, unless accompanied by an R.A.F. officer or a member of one of the ground crews servicing the aircraft. Any unauthorised persons failing to stop when ordered to do so by a guard would be shot.

The first day produced fourteen Italians who had blatantly defied the notices and had been arrested in the vicinity of parked aircraft. Two had nasty-looking bayonet punctures in their buttocks. I kept them in the camp for several hours, during which I carried out repeated interrogations, before allowing them to go free. From then on there were no more strays.

On the far side of the aerodrome an American Constructional group, consisting mainly of Negroes, were building a new runway. They were responsible for their own security, but two days after taking over my new role their Commanding Officer, Colonel Walters, arrived at my office in a state of near panic. A box containing one hundred pounds of dynamite had been stolen and had to be found at all costs, he insisted.

With the four men hand-picked to accompany me on house-raids near the aerodrome, I set off for the American camp. Two of my men were armed with Sten guns, two with rifles and I carried a .300 American carbine.

We were shown the building which had held the dynamite and after some fruitless questioning of the store's personnel set off to tour the camp's perimeter.

At the far end of the new runway I saw a dump covering about one hundred square yards, containing the wrecks of aircraft, badly shot up or otherwise rendered completely unserviceable.

There were two places where entry could be made and the grass around these had been well trodden. As the two entrances were almost exactly opposite each other, I ordered two of my men to mount guard on one while I went to the other with the other two men. I told one guard to shout, in Italian, that the dump was surrounded and that anyone inside should come out with his hands above his head. We listened intently for almost five minutes, but there was no response.

I had almost decided that my suspicions that someone might be in the dump were unfounded when I heard a slight clink of metal on metal coming from a fuselage lying at an angle of about forty-five degrees and jutting out above the level of the main pile.

From a rent in the side I saw the barrel of an Italian carbine protruding and pointing in my direction. Quickly I ducked out of sight, crawled on my stomach for a few yards and came up again with my carbine at the ready.

As I did so the barrel sticking out of the fuselage swung round towards me once more and there was a sharp crack as the bullets spat forth. I threw myself on the ground—in the same movement firing in retaliation. I pumped half a dozen bullets through the thin skin of the fuselage and was rewarded by a scream of pain, a thud and the disappearance of the carbine as it fell back through the hole.

A deathly hush settled over the dump once again—no sound came from the fuselage.

'We are police. Throw out your weapons and come out with your hands raised above your heads,' shouted the Yugoslav who lay beside me, his eyes glittering with excitement.

In reply a hand grenade came flying through the air, well above our heads. I buried my face in the mud as the explosion went off, sending pieces of metal in every direction.

A third warning was shouted to the occupants of the fuselage, but no one came out. Instead, a fusillade of bullets whined over us, some thudding into the ground in front, while others whined away into the distance as they ricocheted off the hulk of an old Wellington standing nearby.

Sufficient warnings and more than enough opportunities for our attackers to surrender had been made. I gave the order to fire. We sprayed the entire length of the fuselage with bullets from my carbine and the two Sten guns. As we systematically repeated the operation an animal-like scream cut through the air and an excited Italian voice pleaded for the firing to stop.

We ceased firing and almost immediately five men and two youths scrambled down from the metal hulk, dragging another man behind them. The two Yugoslavs levelled their weapons in readiness as I went up to our captives. The wounded man was whimpering quietly, his hands clasped over a stomach wound which sent a steady stream of blood running through his fingers. I searched the others, who chattered excitedly that there were two more men inside the pile of broken fuselage and wings.

'But they are dead, signor,' sobbed one man, who seemed almost petrified with fear. 'You will find stolen goods—the stuff you are looking for—it is all in there,' he blurted out. The others glared at him and I saw hatred written on the faces of the two youths.

Leaving the two Yugoslavs on guard, I bundled the Italians into the back of my jeep and drove back to the American camp, the two guards who had missed the excitement keeping an eye on the prisoners. An ambulance was sent for to pick up the wounded man. The Military Police were also summoned to collect the Italians, while I returned to the dump with Colonel Walters, who could barely suppress his pleasure over the arrests. We also took along some of his engineers and a large crane.

The machine was not long in clearing a path towards the centre until we came to the fuselage of a Liberator. Inside lay the body of an Italian, shot through the head, and at the base of the fuselage I had fired at first of all lay another man with two bullet holes in his chest. He was quite dead. Further along the hulk we found the missing box of dynamite, intact, plus a large quantity of engineering parts, removed from heavy machinery, and a considerable stock of American canned food.

When security was back on a normal footing again I soon grew bored with the strict routine that had to be observed, with steadily decreasing results. After smashing up the gang in the dump the Italians grew wary of us and days would go by without an incident. The Yugoslavs were completely reliable and did their work with such fervour and efficiency that it was a brave man indeed who would dare to venture near the forbidden zones without permission.

I requested a transfer back to Dakotas and the transport service into Yugoslavia. When my first assignment came through it was to Bojnik, in Serbia, near the Bulgarian border. This air strip had been used once before and as there was now heavy fighting south of this area, between the Partisans and a force of around two thousand Germans, supplies were urgently required.

A Russian pilot flew the aircraft from Bari, some thirty miles up the coast from Brindisi, and when we landed at our destination we were greeted by the District Commissar, a youth of seventeen. I remarked that he seemed rather young to have such responsibility. Through our interpreter he replied that he had spent four years in Russia, learning how to be a good Communist. On his return he had been chosen as the district's leader. No one could challenge his authority, he emphasised.

The air strip was in a terrible condition—full of holes and furrowed by mud, caked to a cement-like consistency. I requested the Commissar to get the holes filled in and to carry out general surface repair work.

He murmured his assent and set off at a brisk pace to round up the labour force. One hour later he returned with twenty men and ten women. Most of them seemed in their late sixties, a few had definitely seen seventy and about one-third were barely able to walk. He must have noticed the look of amazement on my face, because he was quick

F

to reassure me that they were willing workers and their age meant nothing.

'It is difficult to find strong men nowadays,' he said sadly, as the workers got down to business. 'They are all fighting and leave the old ones behind. These are bad times for us. I would fight too, but you see I must stay behind to look after these people. I have been chosen.'

The Commissar did no work but strode amongst the toiling labourers urging them on by impressing upon them that until the job was finished no more aircraft would land. If this happened there would be no food, no medicine, no guns and ammunition for their fighting men, he kept repeating like a cracked gramophone record.

At lunch-time he led me to a small whitewashed cottage where I was to be billeted. A massive Serb, Jorko, did the cooking and produced steaming bowls of thick soup from a large black pot, filled with boiled mutton and several kinds of vegetables. To wash it down I drank the native brew, rakkia—distilled from plums, damsons and even crab apples.

The meal was barely over when the Commissar returned with an invitation to visit the hospital. We arrived at a large barn and when the door was opened I was nearly bowled over by the stench of human flesh in a state of putrefaction. The twenty wounded lay in two lines on the filthy earthen floor with only bloodstained blankets beneath them and little or no covering on top.

Many were without limbs and others had body wounds. Some of the wounds were quite horrifying and as the bandaging and treatment was extremely crude the men were clearly suffering untold agonies. It was obvious that many of the limbless were in the first stages of developing gangrene.

I told the Commissar that I would do my best to get an aircraft to uplift them that night. He thanked me and rushed off to the air strip to urge the workers into finishing the job.

Back at my headquarters—in a large farmhouse—the wireless operator got the message through and we received word in reply that an aircraft was standing by, loaded with weapons, ammunition and medical supplies. It would take off at 8 p.m.

I went to look for the Commissar and found him strutting up and down the landing strip, where the repair work had been completed. He was pleased with his achievement and his face beamed with pleasure when I complimented him on his efforts.

That evening we rounded up some bullock carts and a shuttle service ran between the barn and the air strip as the wounded were brought down to await the arrival of the aircraft. Although we tried to be as careful as we could when lifting the men in and out of the carts, and on the journey along the bumpy tracks, several collapsed, overwhelmed by shock and pain.

The darkness was intense with only the glimmer of an occasional star breaking the black canvas that was the sky. A wind began to blow, at first a wispy breeze but later increasing in force, driving quick flurries of rain before it. I kept my fingers crossed that conditions would not worsen. I knew that should the rainfall increase it would not take much to turn the air strip into an oozing quagmire of thick, dark mud.

Shortly after 11 p.m. I heard the sound of an aircraft approaching. Whether it was friend or foe was in every-one's minds as the throbbing of the engines drew closer.

When it was directly overhead I breathed a sigh of relief when I saw the downward flashing light signalling to us. I ordered the lighting of the two lines of oil flares, marking the path of the runway, and it was a cheering sight as each one caught fire, the flames burning fiercely in the strong wind.

After a circuit the Dakota landed without trouble. The all-Russian crew were eager to stay as short a time as

possible on the ground and asked for all speed in the unloading of the supplies and the loading of the wounded.

Everyone got down to work with a will—except for
the young Commissar. He stood around, making no effort
to help, until the Russian pilot turned on him. For a full
minute he cursed the startled youth, who, at first, was
arrogant, then belligerent and finally subdued. Without a
word in reply to the torrent of Russian directed at him, he
turned on his heel and strode off to help two old women
who were struggling to lift a wounded man into the aircraft. The job was completed in just under an hour and with
a good deal of cheering and waving the Dakota took off,
the noise of its engines fading rapidly as it disappeared into
the darkness.

For sixteen days I worked with the Yugoslavs in the
Bojnik district and began to form a great deal of respect for
the young Commissar. He had all the impetuousness of
youth and was certainly full of his own importance. But
his sincerity and devotion to duty soon began to show
through and I found that many of the older people liked
and respected him. He was born to lead—all that was
needed was for the rough edges to be smoothed off.

When fierce fighting broke out a few miles from Bojnik
my superiors at Brindisi ordered my recall. Although I flew
to Yugoslavia on many occasions after this, I never returned
to Bojnik. I regretted this, as the villagers in the small
hamlet were first-class people and a deep bond of friendship
had grown up between us.

When the excitement of my flights and parachute drops
into Yugoslavia began to pall I grew restless to be back on
bombing operations once again. I requested a posting to
the Far East and after enlisting the aid of a young squadron
leader in the Postings Branch at Middle East Command in
Cairo, for whom I had previously done a good turn, it was
granted. I was told to return to the U.K. for a refresher
course and some additional training on a new semi-auto-
matic bomb-sight. This would take several weeks; I could

have fourteen days' leave—then I would be free to have the tour of duty in the Far East, which had escaped me two years previously.

My training at West Freugh, near Stranraer, was nearly at an end when, on May 8, 1945, the Germans surrendered. My dreams of the Far East began to fade and had soon vanished entirely when I found myself with a permanent posting to the West Freugh Bomb Trials Unit. Completely bored with the uneventful life, I decided to quit the Air Force when, in September, a memorandum was circulated stating that all personnel who had left reserved occupations to enter the Services could, if they wished, be released to return to their civilian jobs.

When I reported for duty at the Flying Squad office I found very few of my old colleagues left. Ted Greeno was now the chief inspector in charge. Ted, in the minds of the underworld, was the most feared policeman in the Force. He had the most fantastic knowledge of criminals I have ever come across and once he had seen a face he could memorise it and had the ability to recognise it again years later. When he was appointed some years later to the Murder Squad he enhanced his name by gaining the record of solving every murder case he handled.

After a spell on a division and a refresher course at Hendon I was able to return to the work I had loved so well before the war—out in a Squad car with the whole of London as my beat.

There seemed to be even more pickpockets than in pre-war days and many of my cases involved this type of crime. It gave me wonderful experience in specialising in this field and soon I knew every pickpocket known to the police in London, and a great number from the provinces. I was teamed up with Jock Marr, a powerful, broad-shouldered individual, but because of his soft speech was known as 'Quiet Harry'.

Because of an increasing number of complaints pouring in from racecourses, Jock, myself and several other detectives were formed into the Racecourse Squad with orders to clean-up the pickpockets, confidence tricksters and gangs who were frequenting the meetings.

There were five of us—'Flaps' Dawes (thus known because of his big ears), Fred Norris, 'Pedlar' Palmer, Jock Marr and myself. On some occasions one other officer would join us when we required additional help.

Our territory covered every major racecourse in the country and within a few months I had walked on the turf of Ascot, Goodwood, Windsor, Aintree, Doncaster and Newmarket. The larger the race meeting, the greater number of villains would be present in the crowds. Derby Day or the Grand National meeting seemed to bring them out like flies in the first warmth of spring.

One of the neatest and most audacious methods of making easy money was carried out at Epsom one Derby Day. Inside the perimeter of the track, on the Downs, had sprung up a vast collection of charabancs, bookmakers' stands, refreshment tents, jellied-eel stalls, hot-dog kiosks and a thousand and one other methods of extracting money from a public eager to spend. There were also dozens of tipsters gathering vast crowds around them, eager to be told of the 'certain' winner, upon payment of half a crown. Always to the forefront, and perhaps the most famous of all, was Ras Prince Monolulu, a magnificent Zulu, bedecked in equally splendid attire.

In the midst of this motley throng there sprang up a new edifice—a totalisator. It appeared after the first race, complete with paying-in windows and on the front a large red sign announced that 'the very best odds' would be paid to the winning punters. It was an instant hit with the crowds and the money poured in even after the Derby had started.

As the horses thundered round the track and the favourite began to take the lead there were many in the crowd who looked forward to a good sum of money in return for their bets. The race over, hundreds of successful punters began to form long queues in front of the closed windows, waiting for the pay-out.

As time passed they grew more restless and a few of the more impatient knocked sharply on the shutters. But they got no response and the windows remained closed. One man decided to have a look at the back and was flabbergasted to find himself staring into an empty shell. The birds and the money had flown. When he shouted the news to the others pandemonium broke out.

Angry men and equally furious women milled about not quite sure what to do but ready to attack anyone whom they thought even vaguely resembled the men they had seen behind the windows of the totalisator. Although we roamed Epsom, armed with dozens of different descriptions, we never caught up with the phoney operators. Nevertheless the trick was never repeated.

Most of the bookmakers were honest individuals, but occasionally we came up against the crooks among them. We always walked around in pairs and at Epsom on this particular occasion I was with Jock Marr while Pedlar Palmer was teamed up with Fred Norris.

They received a tip-off that a bookmaker was behaving most suspiciously and it was thought he would do a skip when the main race of the afternoon got under way. They watched discreetly from some distance away and saw that the money taken from the punters, instead of going into the bag, was being carefully stowed away in the so-called clerk's pockets. The pseudo-bookmaker was offering much higher odds than his legitimate counterparts and consequently attracted a large amount of business.

When the race started the bookmaker and the clerk climbed down from their boxes beside the board and stood for several seconds glancing about them. Then they were off, disappearing into the throngs of people who stood with eyes firmly fixed on the body of horses galloping round the course.

Pedlar and Fred gave chase and arrested them without

difficulty. While Pedlar set off with his prisoners to the police tent, Fred started to uproot the bookmaker's board, which would be needed as evidence. One punter on the edge of the crowd spotted him in the act. Thinking it was the bookmaker making off with the proceeds, he ran towards Fred, shouting and cursing. His outburst caused many heads to turn from the race. They too saw the red-faced Fred struggling with the board and the man haranguing and pushing him. They rushed to join in the fray. They either ignored or could not hear Fred's explanation that he had just arrested the bookmaker in the act of clearing off. They were incensed with rage and started to beat him up.

Jock and I, hearing the commotion, rushed over to see what was going on. We were joined by two uniformed policemen who battled their way through the mob, which was practically pulling Fred apart. We all shouted as loudly as we could that the man they were attacking was a police-man and somehow or other managed to get the message over. By this time Fred's clothes—or what was left of them —were in tatters. His jacket, waistcoat and shirt had vanished and our arrival had only just saved him from losing his trousers as well. The members of the mob, who still hung around, mouths agape, when they realised what they had done, were given a severe lecture and sent packing.

Back at the police tent Pedlar and the other policemen could not suppress their laughter when they saw Fred arrive, clad only in trousers and shoes. When the full story was told the gales of laughter must have spread across Epsom Downs. Even Fred saw the funny side, but wild horses could not drag him near a welshing bookmaker again.

Although our racing days had their lighter side there were also many occasions when violence was in the air—either being committed or being threatened. For one period book-makers were under the constant threat of numerous gangs, operating a protection racket.

The favourite method of extortion was known as the sponge technique. A member of the gang involved would go round the bookmakers, with a small bucket of water and a sponge. He would offer to wash the slates clean and demand payment of either five or ten shillings for the service. If this was not paid up he would signal other gang members, lurking in the crowd. Then they watched for a suitable opportunity to move in and smash up the bookmaker's stand. This was usually done during the busiest time when bets were being placed, prior to a major race. The pages of the book recording the bets would be torn out and thrown away. In many cases the unfortunate bookmaker would be beaten up.

Ted Greeno received a tip-off from one of his numerous contacts that a well-known East End gang was spoiling for trouble and if all went according to plan there would be a good deal of violence at one of the Ascot meetings.

We knew that this gang had about thirty members and would take a great deal of stopping should a pitched battle erupt. Ted laid careful plans and ordered a large number of detectives and plain-clothes men to move into the area. We arrived at Ascot early in the morning and soon policemen were sprinkled liberally in most corners of the course. As I knew most of the gang members, Ted decided that I should approach the leader and warn him of the consequences of trouble.

I did not feel I was risking trouble by doing this because it was highly unlikely that they would strike down a police officer when he had full knowledge of their identity.

I crossed the racetrack through the tunnel which runs from the Silver Ring to the open ground on the other side. This open part of the course was the area normally used by the gangs operating among the bookmakers, whose stands extended from opposite the Royal Enclosure right along the fence down to the car parks. As I padded along I was followed by several fellow detectives, who walked, casually, and on their own—some reading newspapers, others engrossed in racing journals. I had almost reached the car park when I spotted the gang.

At a quick count I totalled twenty-eight, all walking in small groups. I recognised most of them and when one group of five drew near I stepped in front of them. They too recognised me. As they halted I saw the looks of sullen obstinacy creep over their faces.

Dispensing with courtesies, I asked point blank: 'Where's your boss today, then?'

They looked at each other—a couple grinned, the other three furrowed their brows.

'Who, mate? Who're you looking for then, old son?' asked one character, making no effort to hide the leer around his lips.

'Come on, don't beat around the bush. You know very well who I'm looking for. Where is he?' I repeated.

Again they looked at each other, shook their heads, shrugged their shoulders and made to move on.

I had a quick glance around me and could see some of the other groups talking among themselves and looking over in my direction. At least I was comforted by the sight of a couple of plain-clothes men about thirty yards away on my right. A quick sprint, if trouble developed, and they would be with me.

I had another go, this time addressing one man by his name.

'Come on, Harry, you know who I am talking about. I want to speak to your boss.'

But Harry was having none of this and walked off. The others started to follow suit. I saw one of them stop in his tracks and look past me over my shoulder. I turned round and there was their leader strutting towards me. For one of London's most powerful men he looked the exact opposite —being of medium height and corpulent. His hat was pushed well back on his head and he greeted me with a flash of expensive cuff-links in a superbly white shirt as he offered his hand in greeting.

'Well then, Sergeant . . . or is it Inspector? I never can remember, please forgive me. What can I do for you? Been looking for me, 'ave you?' he asked, his face the model of goodwill.

'For the record,' I answered, 'the rank is constable and let's cut out the pleasantries. You know very well what I'm here for and I know why you're here so don't let's mess around.'

'So you're 'ere for the racing as well, then, Constable,' he said, laying particular stress on the 'Constable'.

I cut him short and delivered my message of warning.

'Now let's get this straight—you're out for trouble today and to hell with your bloody story about attending the races.'

He cocked his head to one side, the look of amusement still on his face. I could see some of his henchmen gathering round trying to listen to what I was saying.

'Chief Inspector Greeno knows all about your plans for today and he doesn't like them—no, he doesn't like them one little bit. I'm warning you, if you put one foot wrong, and that goes for any of your bloody hired thugs as well, inside here today we'll put you and everyone with you behind bars for long enough.'

He opened his mouth, but I butted in again: 'Now shut up. We've never been so serious before and bear this in mind—this warning comes straight from the top. You don't want to cross swords with Ted Greeno, now, do you?'

The smile had gone and his face was now cold, with eyes narrowed to mere slits.

'What bloody right have you got to address me in this way? Get the hell out of my way, copper.' He pushed past me.

I quickly got in front of him again and in no uncertain terms repeated the warning. He walked off without a word and made for about a dozen gang members, standing, with their arms folded, beside the fence. They started to talk among themselves and within a minute the remainder had joined them. For ten minutes I stood and watched them.

During this time more than five dozen plain-clothes men had positioned themselves in a wide circle behind the book-makers' stands and along the railings. But as these policemen were mixed in with the considerable mass of people milling around, the gang could not have known they were there, although, no doubt, they suspected they were being watched.

I saw their boss staring over at me on a number of occasions as he talked. Finally they started to drift off in the direction of the car park. I trailed behind and after some more muttering in a close huddle and a couple of obscene gestures, thrown in my direction, they got into a fleet of cars. One by one the vehicles drove off and their day at the races had come to an end.

Their leader reigned supreme for many years until members of a rival gang attacked him in a West End Street. Both he and his two bodyguards were severely mutilated by some horrific razor slashes and left branded for life.

When I was promoted to detective sergeant there was little difference in my life and duties except for a rise in pay. To my delight I was allowed to remain on the Flying Squad instead of being moved out to a division or posted back to ordinary C.I.D. duties as was normal practice when pro-motion occurred. Ted Greeno was promoted and moved to the Murder Squad and Jock Marr became a detective inspector and transferred. I was now assigned to work with Bob Acott, an ex-bomber pilot and holder of the D.F.C.

In the post-war years there was a considerable traffic in forged American dollars going on in London. A large number of forged notes were found to be in circulation causing a great deal of worry to the senior members of the American Secret Service. Eventually the Flying Squad was called in and Bob and I allocated the task of getting to the bottom of the business.

We paid a call on a reliable informer in the West End who had helped us on previous occasions when his information had led to the arrests of people involved in the smuggling of Swiss watches.

He said he already knew about the forgeries and would do all he could to pick up some information for us. A week went by and we had almost given up hope when the telephone rang. He asked us to a rendezvous in the Premier Club, off Charing Cross Road. This club was a favourite haunt of many C.I.D. officers as well as a considerable number of the criminal fraternity. Dave Hatter and his sister Hattie ran the place and I was already on good terms with them both.

Dave gave me a wave as we entered and over at the bar our informant was waiting. He told us that he had arranged to meet a man the following night and had agreed to buy four hundred American dollars from him. The meeting was to take place in a small car park in Soho at 10.30 p.m.

At 9.30 p.m. Bob and I were seated in a disguised Flying Squad van parked at the corner of a street near the car park. On time a man arrived and stopped at the entrance. He lit a cigarette as he prepared to wait. We slipped out of the van and walked up to him.

'We are police officers,' I said, 'and we have reason to believe that you are in unlawful possession of a quantity of American dollars.'

For a moment he just stared at us, then he put his hand in his coat pocket and produced an envelope, which he handed to me.

'So the bastard shopped me,' he murmured, in a broad Belfast accent.

I opened the envelope and counted out thirty-nine American and one Canadian ten-dollar bills.

At West End Central police station he told me he had bought the bills from a man in a Soho pub and intended to sell them at a profit in Belfast, where he owned three amusement parks. I charged him provisionally with the unlawful possession of the dollars.

Next day he was remanded on bail and Bob and I went along to the American Secret Service Department to check whether or not the notes were genuine. We were not long in getting an answer—thirty were forged, while the remaining nine and the Canadian bill were perfectly genuine. We gave the Secret Service men the suspect's address in London, and they spent a great deal of time interviewing him. He adamantly maintained that the story he had given me was the correct one and that he had been the victim of a confidence trick. He did, however, let slip the name of an American sailor who was later found to be one of the ringleaders in the dollar currency racket.

When the man appeared in court again, on the remand date, we now had him charged with failing to offer ninety United States and ten Canadian dollars to an authorised dealer. The magistrate was told that there was no charge relating to the forged notes as it was believed that the man had been conned. It was also mentioned that he had given valuable assistance to the Secret Service Department. He was fined fifty pounds with ten pounds costs.

Our finest sources of information were the West End prostitutes. If you were able to get one or two of them on your side it could go a long way to making life a great deal easier.

Doris haunted the vicinity of Lisle Street, where she had a small flat, and this was where I first met her. One evening while walking along Lisle Street, after paying a social call on Bill Brennan, the owner of the Falcon Pub in Wardour Street, I heard a muffled scream for help coming from an open doorway.

I ran up the stairs and in a room on the first floor was confronted by the sight of one man striking a girl in the face with his fists, while his companion was smashing the furniture. I wrenched the girl's attacker away from her and struck him a strong blow on the chin, which sent him sprawling to the floor. He lay there unconscious. His companion hung back in a corner and when I approached agreed to make no trouble.

I locked the door and had a look at the girl. Her blouse was torn and there were two ugly bruises on her face. When

she calmed down she told me her name was Doris and that
she was a prostitute. She had picked up one of the men and
taken him to her flat.

When she was unlocking the door the second man ran
up the stairs and pushed his way into the room. While one
man held her, the other took the money from her handbag.
But there was not enough cash for them. Believing there
was more hidden in the flat, they had beaten her up to make
her talk. As an added incentive they had also started to break
up the furniture.

When the two men appeared in court they pleaded guilty
to the charges, which included assault, and each received
two years' imprisonment.

Several months later I was again walking in Lisle Street
when Doris stopped me and invited me up to her flat. Then
she poured out two large whiskies and told me her story.

On the previous evening, she said, she had picked up one
of the members of the Camden Town gang who had been
flashing a large wad of notes.

'He told me,' said Doris, 'that they had just done a
tobacconist's shop and got away with the safe as well as a
quantity of cigarettes and lighters. He said the safe was in a
lock-up garage in Chalk Farm Road and that they were
going to get someone to open it for them.'

'When?' I asked.

'That's it . . . that's why I asked you in here. They're
opening it tomorrow morning,' she replied.

I swallowed my whisky and prepared to leave. She waved
away my thanks.

'I have always wanted to pay you back for the favour you
did me over those two men, Mr. Brodie. Anyway, I doubt
if me boyo from last night will ever remember telling me
anything . . . he was plastered.'

She caught hold of my shoulder and giggled.

'He fancies himself that one, but if he's as big a bungler
when he's out with the gang as he is in bed, then he deserves
to be behind bars.'

At 6 a.m. next morning I sat with my companion, Johnny Franklin, in our disguised Squad vehicle, a small, brown nondescript van, with our eyes peeled on the street in front of the lock-up garage. Three hours later three men arrived on foot and went inside. Leaving our driver to radio the information to headquarters and request the assistance of a police car, Johnny and I got out and tiptoed over to the garage door.

I could hear tapping sounds coming from inside. We stood one on either side of the door, knowing full well that before long someone would look out to see if the coast was clear. We had not long to wait. The door opened outwards and Johnny grabbed hold of it.

I sprang at the startled man and sent him flying back inside the garage. Johnny was right behind me. There in the centre of the floor was the safe with two men bending over it. Part of the back had been ripped off. A large crowbar lay alongside with a hammer and several chisels beside it.

When the men saw us one, whom I recognised as Billy Robson, picked up the hammer and moved towards me. Swiftly I drew my short truncheon.

'Don't be a fool. Put that hammer down—there are four more coppers outside,' I told him.

He hesitated for a few seconds, then angrily threw the hammer on the floor at my feet. His companion, who was bending down to pick up a chisel, changed his mind when he heard my threat. The third member, who had been winded when we charged the door, just sat on the floor holding his stomach.

Johnny picked up the tools, and Billy, growing bold again, asked me who had shopped them. I told him it was the furtive way the three of them had approached the garage door that had drawn our attention to them.

'When we saw you go into the garage we became suspicious,' I said.

For good measure I added: 'Anyway, Billy, we were merely in the street trying to trace a witness in an assault case. You probably didn't see us because we were standing in the doorway of a house, talking to the occupant when you went by.'

They were convinced and I was relieved to know that they remained oblivious to the part Doris had played in the events leading to their capture. They cursed me, however, when they heard the police car drawing up and they realised that I had duped them with talk of their being surrounded.

Three years' penal servitude was meted out to each of them in court five weeks later and for the rest of my Flying Squad days Doris remained a faithful and reliable informant.

G

7

The Battle of Heathrow

'ALL Flying Squad cars and officers to report back to Scotland Yard immediately. I repeat, immediately.' The wireless in our black Wolseley crackled as the voice of the operator went off the air. I acknowledged the call and the driver turned the car round to head us back to headquarters in the shortest time possible.

My companion, Detective Sergeant Bob Acott, who had been reclining peaceably on the back seat, shot forward as the car gathered speed. He tapped me on the shoulder.

'Must be something big on, Allan,' he said in his usual quiet manner. Bob never panicked or became excited when something big cropped up. At least on the surface he was able to present a calm and unruffled appearance. This is the sign of a good detective. No matter how complex or dangerous the situation, you must always keep your head. A show of confidence brings an air of authority—this is what the average man in the street wants to see and this is what he respects when he does see it. No doubt this is why Bob rose to the rank of deputy commander.

He has handled many a difficult case over the years. It was Bob who led the officers who burst into a bedroom in a London hotel to arrest police killer Gunther Podola. Perhaps one of his biggest cases was the A.6 murder—the description given by the Press to the Hanratty case. Although the vicious and coldblooded murder of Michael Gregsten and the violent assault on Valerie Storie first hit the newspaper headlines as long ago as August 24, 1961, the public still talk about it.

Controversy rages. Many fear a miscarriage of justice and some are critical of the manner in which the police brought the accused, James Hanratty, to court. From what I know of Bob and despite what is said, I am sure he was perfectly fair and scrupulous in his handling of the case. When I was with him and he found some lead—no matter how slender —he would follow it through to the end. When he arrived at a conclusion it was only after many hours of painstaking work.

But at 4 p.m. on July 29, 1948, when the call came through to our Squad car, neither Bob's nor my own thoughts were fixed on murder. Our problem was housebreaking. We had just been in a pub. Not for a drink on the quiet, as many people imagine the average detective spends fifty per cent of his time doing, but to meet, and drink with, an informer. Every policeman, whether a detective or a uniformed man, has his informer or grass or snout—call him what you like. They are as necessary to a detective as a rifle is to a soldier.

Informers are the lowest dregs of society, despised by the Squad men and hated by the criminal underworld. It is not courage or a sense of public duty that makes them squeal to the police. They are weak-willed, cowardly men, out for a few pounds and, in most cases, a drink. To them, informing on others is a business. Few become very rich at it. For most the road leads to alcoholism or being crippled or maimed for life after a beating-up from someone they have double-crossed. Some of them end their days as a corpse floating in the Thames, a knife between the shoulder blades or a bullet in the skull.

A rendezvous with an informer is almost always made in a pub. I used to make a point of meeting my contacts just at the morning opening time, if this were possible. Usually there were very few people present in the bar at this time. To the licensee it appeared to be quite a casual meeting.

Nevertheless, most publicans knew what was going on, but in the East End they were the very souls of discretion.

On this day Bob and I left the car parked in a back street near Gardiner's Corner and walked round to a pub known as the Princess Alice, in Commercial Street, in the Stepney district. Mine host in this particular pub was Alfie Harris. There was always a cheery grin on his face and a ready chuckle for a customer's joke, no matter how feeble the attempt to tell it. He was about five foot three inches tall, Jewish and dapper. He was a fearless little man who would stand no nonsense. He drank quite a bit—or at least always seemed to do. I don't think I ever saw Alfie without a glass of gin in his hand. On the other hand he could hold his liquor—not once did I ever see him under the weather.

'What'll you have, Mr. Brodie?' he asked, as he placed his gin glass on a shelf behind the bar.

'Two halves of bitter, Alf,' I answered, as I looked around the room.

In one corner a young man sat reading a newspaper, while nearby an old fellow dozed, a glass of stout on the table in front of him. I saw our man watching us. He was a weedy-looking individual, about forty years old, with thin straggly hair and a pale complexion. He was seated at a table on the far side of the room with a copy of a racing newspaper on his lap.

'You'd better give me another half while you're at it, Alf,' I said, as I turned back to the bar again.

I paid for the drinks and Bob picked up two glasses and strolled across the room. I followed.

'Mind if we sit here?' Bob asked.

Our man looked up sharply and shook his head.

'No, no, guv, help yourself.'

He pointed to the two vacant seats around the table.

He did not have much to tell us. He was working for a gang of shopbreakers who had been busy in the East End on several occasions. At least he was trying to worm his way into their confidence. Mind you, if the shopbreakers' boss thought as much of him as I did then our mutual friend had little chance of being a success on either side. However, he gave his report and I told him to keep on trying. As I rose I passed a ten-shilling note across the table under the palm of my hand. Our informer friend took a furtive glance at it. I could see by the expression on his face he wanted more but did not have the guts to come right out and ask for it.

For the rest of the day we patrolled the area. It was fairly routine work, involving watching for stolen cars, wanted persons and anyone acting suspiciously. Our stint was nearly over when the urgent call to return came through at 4 p.m.

In next to no time we reached New Scotland Yard and swept into the Flying Squad car bay. There we were told to go to the briefing-room. When I pushed the door open there were several Squad men seated inside. All waiting . . . all eager to know the reason for their sudden summons. It was all a bit of an anticlimax, however. A senior officer came into the room and in a few crisp sentences told us to report back again later that evening—at 8 p.m. We were to prepare ourselves for an all-night job, he said.

We trudged away feeling a little let down, but there was eager speculation as to what job was on that would require us—in such large numbers—to be out all night.

At 8 p.m., when we had once again remustered in the large briefing-room, we were given our first clue. We were told to make our way to the B.O.A.C. head office in Great Western Road. The journey was made in closed police vans and on our arrival at the building we made our way up several floors to a large conference room which had been adapted as a briefing room by our senior colleagues.

All our speculations—some wild, some fairly sane—as to the nature of the job were soon satisfied when our chief— Chief Inspector Bob Lee, the officer commanding the Flying Squad—took the stage.

Even the most hardened Squad man drew in his breath when he heard the chief inspector outline the information he had received. An attempt was to be made that night to steal diamonds and gold bullion from a bonded warehouse at London's Heathrow Airport.

'It is believed,' he said, with a look of grim determination on his face, 'that from eight to twelve persons will be involved in the attempt. It is known that several members of the gang possess firearms, but it is not thought likely they will use them.

'Nevertheless, they will be armed with other weapons—of that I am certain,' he emphasised.

We were told that we would not be given firearms but would have to depend on our short wooden truncheons if the going became rough.

Chief Inspector Lee then went over the plans he had drawn up. Swiftly, but laying great stress on important points, he laid the full details before us. Within an hour I found myself, along with eleven other Squad men who had been selected to take up positions inside the warehouse, sitting in the back of a large enclosed B.O.A.C. truck, driven by a Squad man, en route for London Airport.

The journey took about three-quarters of an hour, which was long enough for me. I do not recommend a bullion truck as the most comfortable mode of travel. The truck made its way through the maze of roads that run through London Airport and eventually stopped outside the warehouse. A senior officer told us to sit tight. After a few minutes the vehicle was reversed up close to the small wicket gate set at one side of the huge doors.

A colleague opened the truck door, and swiftly, in single file, we entered the building. When the last Squad man was inside, the three night security guards, employed by the airport authorities to watch the warehouse, scrambled unceremoniously into the back of the truck. With a slight rasping of the gears the vehicle moved away into the darkness and the wicket gate was secured. I looked at my watch: it had taken less than three minutes to complete the change-over.

We then made a systematic survey of the inside of the warehouse. It was not long before we realised that the wicket gate was the only means of entry and exit to and from the building. Most definitely this was in our favour. There were problems, however. Apart from two large wooden crates, standing on top of each other near the wicket gate, there was no other place of concealment within twenty yards.

It would be a difficult spot to cover. Chief Inspector Lee was not one to shirk his responsibilities, all the same. He announced that he would take up position behind the crates. Bob Acott and I were to join him.

Our task would be to seal the exit when every member of the gang was inside and hold it until reinforcements arrived from the rear of the inside of the building and from the platform above the main strongroom.

Divisional Detective Inspector George Davis was chosen to lead the team which would be concealed on the platform. They would signal to us to close the gate when the gang was well and truly caught in the trap.

The next assignment was to go to Detective Sergeant Ted Hewitt and two others. They had to dress themselves in security guards' uniforms and take their places inside the steel cage which embraced the strongroom. Ted was given possession of the strongroom keys and, if the information received proved to be correct, cups of tea, containing drugs, would be delivered at 11.30 p.m. from an airport mobile canteen. They were told that the tea was not to be drunk but they should feign unconsciousness should anybody enter the warehouse.

The remaining officers were posted behind parcel racks at the rear of the inside of the building with orders to keep hidden until the alarm was raised. The stage was set. We now awaited the arrival of the principal players.

From my hiding place I was able to see the wicket gate through an aperture between the crates. My eyes remained firmly fixed on the spot.

The time dragged on until 11.30 p.m., when I heard a vehicle drive up and stop a short distance away from the front of the warehouse. A door slammed and footsteps approached. Quickly, Ted made for the gate. There was a knock.

'Tea,' said a muffled voice from the outside.

'O.K.,' Ted replied. 'Hold on—I'll be with you in a jiffy.'

He opened the gate very slightly and, taking great care not to show his face, took a tray, with three cups on it, from the person on the outside. The footsteps receded and Ted came back into the building again, leaving the wicket gate off the catch, as prearranged.

He went to a water drain and poured out most of the tea, saving only sufficient for analysis at a later stage. He then rejoined his companions inside the strongroom cage and all three took up postures similar to men who had been heavily drugged. The critical time had arrived. No definite time had been given by the informer as to when the raid on the warehouse would take place. It could be within the next half-hour or it might be several hours. No one knew—except the gang.

One hour and twenty minutes later—at 12.58 a.m.—we heard the sound of a heavy vehicle approaching. It stopped and then reversed up to the wicket gate.

There was a scuffling noise on the ground which sounded like men jumping down from the vehicle. A few seconds later I saw the gate move slowly and begin to open. Two men entered, looking around them as they walked into the building. Perhaps I should say two apparitions—not men. They looked grotesque—quite horrible.

They wore ladies' silk stockings over their heads and faces with the feet and heels hanging down in front. Each time they exhaled their breath the stocking feet blew up like balloons, then dropped back flat against their faces again when they breathed in. They went past the crates where I was hiding and made their way over to the strongroom cage. Its three occupants snored on in drugged sleep—or so the men thought. They seemed satisfied because, turning on their heels, they walked back to the wicket gate again and went outside.

Minutes later seven men entered—all disguised in the same hideous fashion. It was impossible to identify them because of their masks. All were armed with a variety of weapons and instruments, ranging from lengths of rubber tubing, loaded with lead, to iron bars and an outsize pair of wire cutters. The only exception was a man who carried a paper carrier bag containing a bottle of water, a bottle of tea, six lengths of rope and adhesive tape.

They went straight to the strongroom cage and entered. Ted and his two colleagues were giving an excellent impression of being unconscious. No sound came from them as they were manhandled by the men. There was still no sound when Ted received a vicious kick in the ribs and a colleague was struck on the back of the head by a violent blow from a heavy cosh.

Two of the gang tied up Ted and his men and stuck adhesive tape over their mouths. They took the keys of the strongroom from Ted's pocket and handed them to a fellow member of the gang. He moved to the strongroom door and fitted a key into the lock.

As he did so Divisional Detective Inspector Roberts, who was perched on the upper platform with George Davis, shouted at the top of his voice: 'We are police officers of the Flying Squad. Stay where you are.'

This was my cue to act. Along with Bob Lee and Bob Acott I rushed to the wicket gate and slammed it shut.

All hell broke loose. There was sheer and utter confusion on the part of the gang. The effect of Detective Inspector Roberts' voice and our action in slamming shut their only means of escape had taken them completely by surprise. They began to run towards me and I heard one of them shout: 'Kill the bastards and get the guns.' They were shouting, cursing and in a total state of panic. I could see the ugly variety of weapons which they held ready for use when they got close enough. Even the man who had earlier carried a paper bag produced a handy-looking cosh from his jacket pocket. All around them Squad men were beginning to converge.

The gang member who was in the vanguard of the rush struck Bob Lee on the head with an iron bar. Poor Bob reeled and staggered backwards. I immediately retaliated and hit his assailant a heavy blow across the head with my truncheon. He fell as if he had been pole-axed. As he hit the floor and lay prostrate his body made a useful (for us) stumbling block for his fellow rogues. Bob Acott and I suddenly found ourselves submerged by the unconscious man's companions who fell over him, bumped into each other and were sent sprawling in all directions in a general state of chaos. All the time the cursing went on and the gang struck out with their coshes and iron bars.

Bob and I lashed out at every head covered by a silk stocking. Some blows connected—others did not. By now the other officers who had been hiding came on the scene and a complete free-for-all developed. Blow upon blow was struck by both sides. Iron bars cleaved murderously through the air and the warehouse rang to the sound of groans, curses, yelps of pain and shouts of anger. When the battle was at its height I caught a glimpse of several of my colleagues on the floor but was relieved to see that as many gang members were also immobile.

The intruders fought to the last man, like rats in a trap. More than once I was sent staggering by blows to the head and body but somehow I managed to keep my feet.

In the end sheer weight of numbers prevailed and the last gang member dropped to his knees with a yelp, then slid down, in the best dramatic fashion, to lie sprawled unconscious on the floor.

I stepped back from the scene of carnage, the sweat pouring from me, and went over to the wicket gate. On opening it the cool night air was a welcome visitor.

I was joined a few seconds later by other Flying Squad officers bearing the unconscious form of yet another member of the gang. He had been acting as a look-out on the outside of the wicket gate. From his peaceful slumber, brought about by a wooden truncheon, it appeared that he had not been the best man the gang could have picked for the job.

We now had eight unconscious rogues in the bag. The ninth member of the gang, another outside man, was arrested later.

As my colleagues got their breath back and looked at the injured—on both sides—lying around on the floor, for some unknown reason my mind flashed back to the finale of a day's grouse-shooting on the Glentanar Hills. I had always loved that moment which came at the end of every shoot when the birds were laid out on the ground and the counting of the day's total began. With this thought still uppermost in my mind I walked over and proceeded to lay out all our victims in an orderly line on the concrete floor. I then unmasked them all. I was most surprised to see that, for the most part, they were completely unknown to me— at least for crimes of violence—with the exception of one man.

The men were all revived and it was pathetic to see them when they recovered consciousness. Instead of the lives of luxury which they had no doubt dreamed about after successfully accomplishing the raid, they awoke, one by one, to a world of shocked reality. Fear and self-pity were in their eyes as they looked up from the cold floor and into the eyes of their opponents in battle.

They were hauled to their feet and bundled into a fleet of Flying Squad cars, which had appeared on the scene as a result of a wireless message. They were taken to the local police station where, after medical attention and interrogation, they were eventually charged with offences which included attempted robbery with violence and assaulting the police.

In the police station they maintained a dazed but resigned attitude. All fight had gone from them. From a swaggering bunch of money-hungry criminals they had been transformed into a rather battered, pathetic group of ordinary men. While the questioning was going on my colleagues and I were licking our wounds.

The total casualty list consisted of Bob Lee, severe head wound and concussion; Detective Inspector 'Jock' Peter Sinclair, a suspected fracture of the arm; Detective Don MacMillan, broken nose and head injuries; and myself, head injuries and multiple bruising. Many of the other officers were cut and bruised and it took quite some time before the patching up operations were completed. There was a brisk run on stocks of sticking plaster.

A check was made on the exact value of the 'treasure' held in the Heathrow warehouse and the final figure showed it to be indeed something worthy of such a well organised raid. The safe held diamonds to the value of £13,900 and in the strongroom there lay £224,000 worth of easily transportable goods. A consignment of gold bullion valued at £250,000 should also have been present. It had been scheduled to arrive on the previous day but the aircraft carrying it had been delayed.

One of the great mysteries to us was why one man had been carrying bottles of water and tea when he entered the warehouse. Surely not for a quiet cuppa during the operation? When we did discover the reason I was quite amazed by the strength of the steps taken by the gang to cover up their tracks after the raid, should it have been successful. The water in the bottles was to have been used to wash out the cups, to eliminate all traces of the drugged tea. The genuine tea would then have been poured into the cups as a substitute.

When the case eventually came before the Central Criminal Court, better known as the Old Bailey, a few weeks later the gang had secured the services of a leading Counsel—a Mr. Mishcon, Q.C., being their senior line of defence.

As they trooped into the high dock I was shocked by the transformation that had come over one of their number. When he had been captured he was six foot three inches tall, powerfully built, with the shoulders of an ox, and a head of thick, jet-black hair.

Now on the day he faced judgement he had been transformed into a shambling, ungainly hulk of a man whose hair was now white—no doubt as the result of shock.

Mr. F. D. Barry, prosecuting Counsel, opened up the proceedings in the usual manner by outlining the case for the police in great detail. But the men in the dock—apart from one—were to maintain a tight-lipped silence. The outside man who had been arrested shortly after the fight in the warehouse was the only one to break the barrier of silence and give evidence on oath.

His story, told with a slight tremor in his voice, was to throw some light on what had transpired prior to the raid.

He told the Recorder, Sir Gerald Dodson, and the packed courtroom, that he had been employed as a loader at London Airport when approaches were first made to him. 'About six weeks ago,' he said, 'I went for a drink with two men and during the course of the conversation told them that I worked at the airport.

'At later meetings I met two more men—one of whom looked like a boxer. One night one of them asked what chance there was to get a job at the airport. He wanted a driving job.'

The witness continued: 'He had been at London Airport to get a parcel for his boss, from the B.O.A.C. bond. He asked me what was in the big safe. I told him all the valuables were kept in there. They wanted to know all the details about the airport.

'I said, "Suppose I go to the police and tell them what has been going on?" They said, "You would not live long to enjoy it." I was then asked what time the gold plane came in. I then told them all I knew about the airport and they then told me they were going to rob the place of gold and were the biggest gang in London. I was warned that if I squeaked to the police they would carve me up.'

Immediately after evidence had been given by the officers concerned in the case, Counsel for the Defence intimated that his clients wished to change their pleas from 'not guilty' to 'guilty'.

This was followed by a lengthy haranguing match between Counsel, each one emphasising that a certain amount of leniency should be shown to the accused in view of the punishment meted out by the Flying Squad officers on the night of the raid. When the Recorder spoke he described the raid as 'The Battle of Heathrow'. He added, 'A raid on this scale profoundly shocks society. All you men set your minds and hands to this enterprise. You were playing for high stakes. You went there with a van to carry it out and you went there armed.'

He continued: 'It is difficult for me under these circumstances to accept the suggestion that the plan here did not involve contemplating violence. If that were so, why carry weapons? If this drug had been successful no violence would have been done, but if the drugging were not successful a different set of circumstances would arise. You made sure of your position by being ready for any situation with weapons of all kinds. That is the gravity of the offence.'

He paused and looked around the courtroom. I could see some of the gang looking down uneasily at their feet.

'The charge against you, to which you plead guilty,' he continued, 'is being armed to rob. It does not matter that the actual property was a bunch of keys. They were the keys to the situation and to the safe.

'A raid of this kind is a thing honest people regard with terror and great abhorrence and they expect the law to vindicate honest people and punish those who have done wrong.'

Sir Gerald then went on to uphold the action taken by the Squad men and his stern words of warning to the men in the dock must have cheered the hearts of policemen up and down the country when they read their morning papers the following day. Perhaps today we need more judges of Sir Gerald's calibre—men who will speak out in fierce condemnation of criminal activities and who are prepared to back up this condemnation with sentences to match the words.

The Recorder continued: 'You went prepared for violence and you got it. You got the worst of it and you can hardly complain about that. You were the attackers in the first instance inasmuch as you went to this warehouse. It was you who were going to attack the warehouse and anyone who was there.

'It is of no great assistance to me to have pointed out that you got the worst of this. One can only describe this as the Battle of Heathrow. For that is what it degenerated into— a battle and nothing else.'

The records of the men in the dock were then read out. They rose to their feet, one by one, as their names were called and Sir Gerald passed sentence. The heaviest term of imprisonment was twelve years. Another man got eleven years.

When ten years in jail was meted out to the white-haired member he slumped forward, clutching the front of the dock. Then he collapsed in a dead faint.

Nine years went to two more while another two received eight years each. One man, in view of his previous clean record, was given five years' penal servitude and the gang member who had given evidence and taken no active part in the actual offences in the warehouse was discharged.

One by one the prisoners disappeared down the steps leading from the dock to the cells beneath the court. The semi-conscious man was supported on either side by two prison warders. So closed the crime of the century, up to that date, as far as armed robbery was concerned. It was to be fifteen years before another criminal operation, using a large gang working with military precision, was mounted on such a scale. This time even higher stakes were involved when the Great Train Robbery took place but unfortunately for the Buckinghamshire police there was no tip-off to help them put a spanner in the works. Crime was to become much better organised as the years went by.

I left the court feeling pleased with myself, and I know this feeling was with my colleagues as well. It had been a job well done. We had smashed the most powerful gang in London and if anything called for a celebration this was it.

The tills in St. Stephen's Dive, next door to New Scotland Yard, were busy that night as members of the Flying Squad and local C.I.D. officers who had fought the Battle of Heathrow—and won—raised their glasses in a victory toast.

8

Twenty Good Men and True

'THE Commissioner of Police would consider the release of a limited number of experienced C.I.D. and Special Branch officers who wish to volunteer for service with the Federation of Malaya Police. Officers selected will be given gazetted rank . . .'

This paragraph in the Police Orders caught my eye as I sat in the C.I.D. office at Hackney sipping hot, sugary tea from a cracked mug on a cold December morning in 1950. The London fog lay like a grimy blanket over the city.

I had been transferred to Hackney after an order came into effect that no officer was to be allowed to serve more than three years in the Flying Squad. This was to give greater opportunities of Squad work to a larger number of detectives. I had served six years in this field, counting my pre-war service, so I was one of the first to go.

I never relished the life of a detective attached to a police station. Apart from the occasional interesting case, the daily routine of investigating petty thefts and small-time burglaries bored me to the point of distraction. I missed the excitement of duty in the Squad cars—the never-ending variety of all that went with the job.

In Malaya the country was locked in a fierce struggle to resist the infiltration of Communist terrorists. Since the Declaration of a State of Emergency in 1948, the Communists had made their presence felt in alarming proportions.

No matter how many troops were sent out from Britain to assist in the fight, the number and intensity of terrorist attacks on trains, rubber plantations, and anything else remotely connected with British colonialism, were increasing day by day.

I wanted excitement. I thought, ruefully, that I might get more than I bargained for in Malaya, but I knew I would never stop regretting it if I passed this opportunity over. Twice before I had been thwarted from seeing the Far East—perhaps the third time I would be lucky.

Without further hesitation I pulled forward the old typewriter and made out my application.

Less than three months later, on March 1, 1951, in the company of three other policemen, I was aboard a Constellation heading east via Stuttgart, Cairo, Bahrein, Karachi and Colombo to land at Singapore Airport. I now held the rank of superintendent.

When the door was opened and I stepped on to the gangway to leave the aircraft the tremendous heat hit me like a massive punch. Before I had crossed the tarmac and entered the airport buildings my thick British tweeds were already sticking to the sweat running down my back and chest.

A Malayan inspector was there to greet us and whisk us away to the naval base at H.M.S. *Terror*, a portion of which was being used by the Malayan police as a transit post for policemen coming from, and going back to, Britain.

Next day we were issued with several items of equipment, which included a .38 automatic pistol. We were also advised on what items of clothing we would have to purchase for our uniforms—bush jackets, K.D. shirts, slacks, etc.

As we explored a small portion of Singapore city in search of tailors' shops there seemed to be people everywhere. The pavements were thronged with hurrying figures and streets packed with cars, buses, taxis and tri-shaws. Even in London I had never imagined there could be so many people in one spot at the same time.

I rubbed shoulders with Chinese, Indians, Malays, Tamils, Eurasians and occasionally the odd European, caught up in the madding crowd, and wondered how on earth I would ever be able to tell one Chinese from another—they all looked the same to me. The women—at least the younger ones—were extremely attractive, with high cheekbones and long dark eyelashes, although I was disappointed to see that they nearly all wore European clothes and not, as I had imagined, seductive cheongsams.

The young men were also slim and to a man wore a sort of unofficial uniform of slacks, or tight-fitting shorts, and white open-necked shirts. Many of the older men and women were merely skin and bone, their faces the colour of faded parchment and just as wrinkled. When my afternoon shopping expedition was over I had reached the conclusion that even the Indians and Malays were going to cause me the same bother of identification.

I had only to wait in Singapore for two days before my posting came through—to Alor Star in Kedah, one of the most northerly states in Malaya, and one with a long common boundary with Thailand, where, it was believed, many of the terrorists had their base camps, which they used for making raids across the border.

With three other policemen I set off on the long train journey, crossing the causeway which links Singapore with the mainland of Malaya at Johore Bahru. Due to the large number of attacks on trains during the previous months, resulting in dozens of derailments, our rate of progress was slow and tedious. The terrain was unchanging—dense green jungle down to the side of the track with an occasional clearing, housing a small township with patches of cultivation and the usual coconut palms, or mile upon mile of rubber plantations.

After eight hours we reached Kuala Lumpur, the capital city, where I was told that I would have to stay the night. The train from the north had been ambushed during the night—the engine had been blown off the rails and several carriages had been almost totally destroyed by fire. In addition there had been a considerable number of casualties. Because of the remote spot chosen by the terrorists for the attack, the repair job was a long and arduous one for all concerned.

I was disappointed with the sudden change in my plans, but my despondency soon left me when I was taken to the Station Hotel, a few paces from the white-painted station, and royally entertained by a number of fellow officers, eager to hear some first-hand news from Britain.

In the morning the line was open and, saying goodbye to my three travelling companions who were destined for another region, I boarded the train for my lone journey north. Before we pulled out of the station I had a look at the armoured car fixed to the train. It looked like a giant tank on railway wheels with a turret and several apertures in the sides for machine guns and other weapons. Manning this metal fortress were several cheery-looking Malay policemen.

On the way north we passed the casualty of the previous day, the locomotive and several carriages lying on their sides with hordes of armed policemen on guard. Further along the line at different points there were plenty of other wrecks—savage reminders of other violent ambushes.

At Alor Star, the State capital, a constable was waiting to drive me the seven miles to the police mess, near the landing strip at Kapala Batas. The mess was a long wooden building, raised on stilts, with one floor. It was a dismal place, with seven small bedrooms and an equally small dining-room and lounge. A middle-aged Chinese and his wife looked after everybody, cooking and cleaning as well as attending to a variety of other tasks.

The man was in the process of lighting the paraffin lamps when I entered and his welcome was a smile of gold-capped teeth. As the building seemed to be totally deserted I enquired about the rest of the inhabitants.

'There is only you, sir, and one other—Mr. Love.

But he has been called out—some constables have been killed.'

He adjusted the wick on the lamp, then looked me straight in the face.

'Sir will not object I hope . . . but when will this killing stop? We lived through the killing in the war and now we are faced with more. I am not sure what is happening.'

'You're not the only one,' I told him. 'All you can do is hope. We have many policemen and troops fighting now, but we must wait—it will take time.'

'Perhaps Sir is right,' he said without much enthusiasm as he picked up my luggage and showed me to my room.

Several hours later my fellow occupant, Andrew Love, returned and was able to tell me what had happened.

Earlier in the day two open lorries, carrying special constables from Changlun to the Sintok tin mine, had been ambushed. The road they had been travelling on was extremely rough and cut through an area of dense jungle. It was notorious for ambushes. Fourteen of the twenty constables in the trucks had been killed, slaughtered by the first murderous hail of bullets which riddled the wooden sides of the vehicles. There had been no chance to retaliate and the remaining six did the most sensible thing by jumping out and escaping into the jungle.

Of all who suffered during the Emergency, the special constables had the rawest deal of all. They had the most thankless job in the Force, and for their efforts were the poorest paid. They were the backbone of the earlier-named jungle squads, later known as field forces, making dangerous sorties far into the heart of jungle territory, where the only other humans likely to be encountered were Communist terrorists. In addition, they guarded rubber estates, tin mines, villages, jungle outposts and forts. Sometimes the married men were separated from their wives and families for months on end and all this for the paltry sum of one hundred Malayan dollars (about £12) per month.

After Andrew had finished telling me his story I asked

him why, if the road where the constables had met their
death was such a notorious one, were they not given the
protection of armoured vehicles when going on patrol? He
replied that it was almost impossible to obtain one—the
armoured vehicles in the country were mostly reserved
exclusively for military use.

'You'll have to put up with the use of an ordinary police
car, a jeep or an open truck, I'm afraid. That's how the
police get around here,' he said.

I remarked that it seemed a senseless state of affairs, and
he agreed. It appeared, he told me, that the administration
had so far resisted all attempts at giving too much of a
military look to the police force.

'Bloody bungling politicians,' was the only remark I
could think of in reply to his remarkable statement.

Next morning I went to the State police headquarters in
Alor Star and met the Chief Police Officer, Neville Godwin.
He was a tall, powerfully built man with years of experience
in Malaya and after an introductory chat took me along
to see Tom Slattery, the officer in charge of the Special
Branch, whom I was to assist.

The work consisted of studying captured Communist
documents in an attempt to sift out any clues which might
lead to identifying Party members and possible location of
terrorist camps. Anything really worth while in this line
was rare, as the terrorists had a tight grip on the civilian
population. The Chinese were either sympathetic to the
movement or in such a state of terror, due to the
threats instilled into them, that they shied clear of police
officers.

In order to subject the civilians to their will the terrorists
would warn a father that if he did not help them then
members of his family would be killed. Occasionally, in
order to punch home the message, a village would be
swooped on and an entire family wiped out, leaving the
remaining inhabitants even more determined than before to
have nothing whatsoever to do with the Europeans. As the

Communists tightened their hold more intensely, the atrocities grew more savage.

There were estimated to be around five thousand full-time members of the Communist Party operating from jungle hide-outs at this time, plus a large number of part-time members. The part-timers would leave their wired-in resettled village in the morning, ostensibly to work in the rubber plantations, then slip off to where weapons were concealed. They would then set off to a previously planned ambush spot, either on a roadway or on the railway, and carry out their attack. It was relatively simple for them to return, hide their weapons once more, and get on with their rubber-tapping work.

Due to the vast size and remote location of most of the rubber plantations there was little chance of the workers being found missing from their work, laying them open to having to answer awkward questions on their return. So relentless was the terrorists' hold on them that for a period almost every civilian worker was a possible suspect.

Apart from this vast force, actively engaged in the jungle, there was believed to be at least eighty thousand active sympathisers who supplied food, money and information to the Communists. Information of troop and police movements was of vital importance to the terrorists, as it enabled them to keep tabs on the strength and deployment of security forces, giving them ample opportunities to plan ambushes and put them into effect. When an attack was made on a rubber plantation the terrorists knew exactly what they would find and what opposition they were likely to encounter.

Some of the braver souls among the civilian population did talk, providing valuable information resulting in a substantial number of kills being made against terrorist bands.

However, in some cases the information they passed to us was so blatantly obvious anyway that we were led to believe that certain Communists had outlived their useful-ness and were being deliberately sacrificed by hired informers in order to rid the movement of men or groups whose loyalty was in question.

This, then, was the massive task facing the security forces and in particular the Special Branch, whose job it was to find, sift through, and analyse the information obtained. We had to be extremely careful. The terrorists used great cunning in setting up situations where a villager—usually a shopkeeper or some minor official in the local council—would be arrested and pour forth a story giving details of hide-outs in the locality which at first sight would seem to be a godsend to us. In a few instances this information was acted upon with all possible speed, there being no time to check out all the facts.

A jungle force would be sent out to investigate. As they approached the area, pin-pointed for us by our willing informer, they would find themselves walking straight into a trap. The ambush normally took place in a part of the jungle which was particularly thick and grown over with foliage. Without warning they would be greeted by a barrage of bullets, followed up by a hail of grenades. On several occasions entire forces were wiped out, but after several incidents when there were survivors able to make their way back to tell the story of what had happened we grew wary of much of the information given to us. Before following any lead we subjected the informant to intense and unrelenting interrogation until we were absolutely satisfied that he, or in some cases she, was telling the truth.

The main source of recreation in Alor Star was attendance at the Kedah Club, which boasted a golf-course, billiards room, badminton and tennis courts, a dance floor, and—for many the most important of all—a large lounge-bar. Much of the leisure time of the small European community was centred on this spot, not so much because they were hardened drinkers but because it was about the only place where they could all relax together and talk over the general situation affecting them all. In common with bars in most clubs, it could also be the main centre for the passing on of gossip—

much of it harmless, but now and again reaching serious proportions.

Many of the members were either bachelors or men with their families in Britain, partly because of the housing problems and partly because of the Emergency. There were no schooling facilities, which meant that if a wife did accompany her husband the children had to be left behind. To any closely knit family this was a highly unsatisfactory arrangement and led in a number of cases to serious domestic difficulties.

By the end of my first month with the Special Branch I found myself growing restless and impatient. I found the task of reading and re-reading the scraps of information that came my way growing more monotonous as each day went by. All of the documents were written in Chinese and had to be passed through the hands of an interpreter before they reached either Tom or myself. Most of them proved to be worthless and in the few cases where we did get on to something worth while the job of following it up was passed on to other policemen. I wanted to get out and about —to do as I had done so often in London—to find the information and see the operation through to its final conclusion.

Apart from this frustration I was growing tired of sitting in my office in a rattan chair sweating like an ox, due to the heat and humidity. A large electric fan spun round above my desk, but was completely inadequate for the task of providing cool air. When turned down it only succeeded in sending the hot air from one part of the room to the other and when switched full on would send the papers and cigarette ash flying from the desk, with severe effects on my temper.

At last I could stand it no longer and decided to broach Neville Godwin and request a transfer to a more attractive existence. My opportunity came one night in the club bar when an impromptu session was under way. Neville asked me how I was settling down. I bluntly told him I wasn't happy and wished to go on jungle duties.

'You must be joking,' was all he could think of in reply.

I assured him I had never been more serious and explained my difficulties. The Deputy Chief Police Officer, Bobby Hicks, who was standing nearby and overheard our conversation, agreed with me, adding that the Special Branch was no place for any officer who did not have a flair for office work. Neville agreed to release me for field work and I was told I would be given several sorties to lead, in order to see how I shaped up. He then foolishly placed a wager of a bottle of whisky with me that I would not last a month in the jungle and would soon be requesting my old job back again. I readily accepted the challenge and was so delighted with my success that I bought many rounds of drinks as the evening wore on.

Next day I paid a visit to the equipment stores and drew several jungle-green uniforms, a haversack and a Mk. V rifle.

In those early days the stock of firearms available to the police was limited, with one Bren and two Sten guns being issued to a platoon of thirty men. The remainder of the men carried .303 rifles, many of them an early vintage.

Two days later the operations officer gave me my first assignment. Information had been received that several terrorists were using a cave as a hide-out near the summit of Gunong Perak, a steep mountain which rose out of the jungle north of Alor Star. The terrorists were believed to be members of a band responsible for an attack on a police post which had resulted in the death of two special constables and the severe injury of several others. The cave had been used by two Malays, in pre-Emergency days, as a shelter when they went out on honey-gathering expeditions. One of them had returned to it only a few days previously and found signs of it having been used by several Chinese.

The Malay was positive of their identity by scraps of food and other small items found lying on the earthen floor. He flatly refused to accompany the patrol back to the spot and pointed out that there was only one faint path that could be used to reach the cave. Furthermore, he was unable to help in pointing out on a map the starting point of the path. I drew half a dozen grenades from the store, in case the terrorists barricaded themselves in, and set off to meet my platoon at Alor Star police station, where I was told five days' rations would be available for our use.

Twenty men—all Malays—stood smartly to attention, and apart from one corporal, who could speak a few words of English, they had great difficulty in understanding me, as I had only a slight smattering of the Malay language.

Things were growing extremely complicated, with my men beaming all over their round, dusky faces, but completely unable to grasp my conversation, when an English-speaking Malay inspector came on the scene. With his assistance I explained the purpose of the operation.

As we talked I studied them carefully. If ever teamwork was more essential it was deep in the heart of the jungle, especially during the hours of darkness when each man had to feel certain that he could depend completely on the others who were with him.

The Malays were all good-natured, and apart from four who were taller than was usual, the remainder were around five foot four inches in height and stockily built. The Bren gunner, who was introduced as Osman, bubbled over with good humour. He was only about five foot three inches tall but barrel-chested with massive shoulders.

We set out in two trucks and, after travelling to Pendang by road, branched off along a rough and bumpy track to a small kampong. From there we went on foot. In single file we crossed an expanse of paddy fields, the fierce tropical sun beating down relentlessly, soaking my jungle greens in sweat and making the 30 lb. haversack on my back feel like a ton weight. As we entered the area of secondary jungle at the foot of the mountain it was a relief to be out of the furnace and walking in the cool damp air.

Giant trees reared skywards, the thick foliage at the top intertwining with other trees to shut out most of the light.

Birds called, and now and again I saw small families of monkeys peering down at us from the trees. As they saw me look up at them they chattered among themselves, then, screeching noisily, disappeared to a higher vantage point. Occasionally a gap in the tree-top growth sent a bright shaft of sunlight through the dim atmosphere—the beam acting like a searchlight in reverse.

A short distance ahead were my two scouts carrying out a reconnaissance of the terrain and always on the alert for possible signs of terrorists in the vicinity. I was soon aware of a feeling of tension in the air. The jungle had the depressing effect of making one feel claustrophobic. The deep undergrowth and the trailing creepers, coupled with the dim light, made it difficult to believe that outside the sun shone brightly and the air was pure, though hot.

After ten miles we reached a clearing with the welcome sight of a small stream trickling through it and I decided to call a halt and make camp for the night. My scouts reported that there did not seem to be any terrorists in the near vicinity, so I considered it safe enough to light a fire. Soon the smell of cooking filled the air as the rice, mixed with curry powder and pilchards in tomato sauce, bubbled around in a couple of small pots. This may sound a peculiar dish, but after a tough six-hour march it was a gourmet's delight to us. The mixture was washed down with several cups of sweet tea.

While the corporal read out the roster for sentry duty I went to the stream, stripped off and washed myself down from head to feet. As the sweat and grime left me and the icy water tingled the pores of my skin I felt refreshed and completely content. Not since the days of my youth had I felt like this. There had been many occasions when after a hard day on the moors hunting stags I had swum in the crystal-clear waters of a mountain stream to wash away my tiredness.

Now for the first time since those happy days I was again out in the open air and enjoying it, although this time the responsibilities were much greater, and, unlike stags, those whom I hunted could strike back.

When I looked round the clearing and saw my men settling down for the night, fully clad with their rifles by their sides, and two of their companions standing guard on either side of the clearing, I knew that Neville Godwin could say goodbye to his bottle of whisky. My mind was made up—this was the life I wanted.

I settled down to sleep in my basha (shelter), which consisted of a piece of plastic sheeting, bought from a Chinese merchant in Alor Star, slung over a piece of rope tied between two trees and tethered at the four corners. This primitive construction would shed the heavy morning dew or protect me from rain should a fierce shower pelt down during the night. A ground-sheet kept out the ground's dampness and I slept fully clothed, wrapped in two blankets. My final touch was a mosquito net draped over the basha.

Despite the high-pierced whine of the mosquitoes as they searched the clearing for fresh blood to suck and the hundred and one other insect noises, I must have dropped off to sleep in a matter of minutes. I knew nothing until I woke up eleven and a half hours later at 6.30 a.m., to the sight of a large mug of tea being brandished in front of me by Osman, the cheery Bren gunner.

After breakfasting on a small piece of cheese from one of the ration tins and a few hard biscuits it was time to set off once more. We were now near the area where our Malay informant had spoken of the path up the mountain-side. For an hour we hunted in all directions without success. The undergrowth was thick and unbroken and I could see no signs of any part of it having been trampled.

From where I stood, having called off the search in order to let my men rest their aching legs, I could see right up the mountain, which was sheathed in dense jungle almost to the summit. Near the top and to the right was a large outcrop of rock. According to my information this was the area in which the cave was situated. It looked impregnable, the huge rocks jutting out into space without any sign of a way to reach them.

I decided to set off towards them, working at an angle up the shoulder of the mountain. Calling the men to their feet, we set off. The climb was more difficult than I had first imagined. Dozens of obstacles barred our way, from fallen trees and thick trailing creepers, some with stems the thickness of my arm, to large boulders which refused to budge. We took turns to hack a path through the foliage, using our machettes until the sweat ran in torrents down our faces and necks. Every few hundred yards I halted the column and we stood listening for sounds of other men making their way through the forest. When we were on the move with the machettes biting and slashing into the undergrowth it sounded to me as if an entire army was on the march instead of a body of twenty-one men. But when we listened there was nothing to alarm us, the only sounds being the humming of the insects and the occasional squawk of a bird as it foraged for food.

It was slow going and at the end of four hours we had only covered about one thousand feet. After a half-hour rest, some cold rice and a drink of water, we were on the move again. The undergrowth grew less dense and after a time the machettes were no longer required.

I brought the column to a standstill as I saw the corporal, who was in the lead, raise his hand to signal he had found something. I went forward and he pointed to an area of ground where the grass was trampled and the creepers broken and twisted. Together we explored a little further and found the start of the elusive path. From what I could see, it led straight up the remaining part of the mountain.

Cautously we went forward, our weapons cocked and ready. If the terrorists knew of our presence in the locality then this was the spot in which they would most likely attempt to kill us. After an hour we reached the base of the rock outcrop. The entrance to the cave lay half-way up and off a ledge, which twisted and turned as it shelved its way round the rocks.

Taking five men with me, including Osman and the man he used to feed the magazines to him when his Bren gun was in action, I slowly climbed up on to the ledge. The final swing upwards was the most difficult of all, as it meant hanging in mid-air for a fraction of a second while I swung my body forwards and up. The first man up helped the next, with his rifle and other equipment, until all six of us were perched on the narrow shelf of rock.

Leaving the Bren team, I crawled along on my stomach, clutching the .38 in my right hand and a grenade in the other. Behind me, with their rifles, came the other two Malay constables. About thirty feet round the ledge I found myself looking into a deep recess in the rock face. It appeared to go far back into the depths of the mountain.

We lay there, still and silent, for almost twenty minutes, but no sound came from the cave. When I looked to my left I could see for miles, far down into the valleys and across the jungle which stretched away as far as the eye could see. A blue haze hung over the trees and the reflection of the harsh sunlight on the white rocks began to dazzle me. I looked over my shoulder and signalled to the two Malays who lay like statues—the only sign of their being alive was the quick flick of their heads as they brushed away an annoying fly as it buzzed around the sweat on their foreheads.

Inch by inch we moved forward until at last we were inside the entrance. Again we lay for what seemed like hours, although it could not have been more than fifteen minutes, as our eyes became accustomed to the darkness. Gradually vague shadowy objects began to assume shapes and eventually I was satisfied that no one was at home—at least not lying sleeping near the mouth.

I rose to my feet and instantly the two Malays were at my side, their rifles levelled and pointing into the black chasm that stretched away in front of us. Again we moved forward, stopping every so often to listen for any sound of danger. About seventy-five feet from the entrance the cave stopped abruptly—a massive fall of rock had obviously blocked the passageway for some time. I searched the floor for tell-tale signs of recent use but apart from some wood embers of indeterminate age there were no other signs of life.

It was now afternoon and too late to make the difficult descent of the mountain before dark. I decided to make camp in the cave. If any terrorists were around and sought shelter for the night they would be in for a nasty shock when they found a platoon of policemen holed up in their former home.

As the cave was situated on the north side of the peak I decided to explore, in the morning, the eastern side and make our descent in this direction.

We had not travelled far before I began to regret my decision. Thick, tough undergrowth barred our way and although we hacked and cut at it for over an hour we only managed to travel three hundred feet. Although sorely tempted to turn back, we pressed on and without warning found ourselves in a cleft in the side of the mountain.

It was a dry watershed down which in the monsoon season would rage a cascading torrent of water. Now there was not even a trickle. As the undergrowth was dense on either side, we started to descend over the rocks and boulders. We found the going fairly easy and made good progress until we were halted by the watershed falling away in a series of large steps. The problem of overcoming this obstacle was soon solved by one of the constables who, together with some willing helpers, cut several long slender trees, growing at the side of the ravine. Placing these over the steps we were able to crawl down them without too much difficulty.

When we were within three hundred feet of the bottom a tree growing out of the rocks spanned the next step down, which appeared to be a green mossy piece of flat rock. I went down the trunk first and about six feet from the rock

Police Lieutenant Underwood teaches members of the Sakai aborigine tribe to shoot . . .

. . . and makes friends with their women and children

Sir Gerald and Lady Templer inspect schoolchildren during the High Commissioner's farewell tour of Malaya

This crocodile, caught by Malay villagers, was brought to the local police station for disposal—still very much alive!

decided to drop down the rest of the way. When my feet touched it I found there was no solid substance underneath and that I was plunging through it. For a few seconds I fell, in utter darkness, until I found myself bumping down the face of a rock. I could feel the skin being torn from every part of my body that came in contact with the jagged stones.

With an abrupt crash I stopped falling and lay spread-eagled at the bottom of what appeared to be a deep tunnel. I began to feel my legs and arms for signs of broken bones and at that moment remembered the hand grenade which had been clipped to my belt. I put my hand to my waist. The grenade had gone.

The force of my descent had torn it away, but somehow or other the pin must have remained intact.

I found I was sitting on a small ledge and that the tunnel dropped away, at an angle, to a small patch of daylight about twenty feet below. Carefully I wormed my way towards it and squeezed through the narrow gap between two rocks to find myself on another narrow ledge with a second menacing drop, this time into hundreds of feet of space, on the left.

I could hear hushed voices from somewhere above my head. Painfully I craned my neck backwards to look up. About forty feet above me a row of worried faces peered down—it was my Malay constables, obviously discussing among themselves the rapid disappearance of the tuan. The grins came back to their faces when they spotted me, although I must have looked a dreadful sight, covered in blood from head to toe and my clothing in ribbons. It took them several minutes to work their way down to join me. They all showed great concern over my wounds and were surprised to see that I was still clutching my rifle. So was I.

When we reached the foot and made camp, beside a small trickle of water, I sponged my numerous gashes and, with Osman's assistance, bandaged up the main flesh wounds

I

in my head, arms and legs. By the time I fell asleep I felt back to normal again. But in the morning it was a vastly different story. I awoke with an ache in every muscle and bone in my body. My clothing stuck to raw flesh. I forced myself to drink some hot tea, although it almost made me sick to even think of swallowing it. With two constables carrying my equipment, we struck out on the second stage of our return journey.

As I walked I found myself suffering periodic bursts of light-headedness and the Malays looked anxiously in my direction as I staggered and almost fell on numerous occasions. Whenever this happened a man was quickly at my side, ready to catch me if I pitched forward on my face.

I was practically all in when we reached the spot where we had camped on our first night out. As I lay in my basha there was little peace. By now the gashes had started to suppurate and the sweat running into them had made them red and angry-looking. The dozens of grazes, which had seemed of no consequence the previous night, now began to take on an alarming look as they reddened and started to fester. Throughout the night I tossed and turned and when the cold light of day broke over the jungle a fever had started to gain control over my body.

I was anxious to press on while I could still walk, and the final ten miles to Pendang police station were miles of sheer and utter torture. A telephone call from the station brought our transport and within an hour I was in a hospital bed at Alor Star.

For two days I tossed and turned and the doctors and nurses pumped endless quantities of penicillin into my arms, hips and legs. On my second night I felt much better and by the third day was making a perfect nuisance of myself, demanding to know why I was being kept in bed when there was nothing the matter with me. I was considerably cheered up when I had a visit from the entire platoon—each bearing a small gift which I was sure they could ill afford.

I was touched by their kindness and I am sure that these policemen were responsible for ingraining into me the affection I was to have for the Malay race in years to come.

Like everyone else they had their own human weaknesses but I never found one who let me down.

9

Baptism by Bullets

By the middle of 1951 a great deal of resettlement, which mainly affected the Chinese squatter population, had been completed. These squatters were spread all over the countryside and made excellent contacts in the supply of food and information to the terrorists.

Following a plan prepared by the Administration's civil servants, which had become known popularly as the Briggs Plan, these people were re-grouped into villages in a central area. Each settlement was closely guarded and surrounded by a high barbed-wire fence. A police post was established in each and look-out towers built at strategic points around the perimeters.

Commendable as it was, the plan was only a partial success. This was due to two factors. In the first place insufficient numbers of police were provided to carry out the guard duties, and, secondly, the Administration failed entirely to take stock of the human element.

Many of the Malay special constables hated the darkness and kept their patrolling of the perimeter fences down to an absolute minimum. Any potential food-suppliers had little difficulty in keeping watch on the movements of these patrols. It was therefore a simple matter for them to slip away from one of the buildings and deposit a parcel of food on the outside of the fence at a time previously arranged with the terrorists. When the coast was clear the Communists left the surrounding cover, picked up the packages and were gone without the guards being any the wiser.

The police posts were simply sandbagged wooden buildings, standing on stilts, with a trapdoor leading down to slit trenches. In each of the look-out towers—normally there were four, occasionally more depending on the size of the village—were two constables. On many occasions, usually in the early hours of the morning, a small marauding band would attack a post, swiftly and silently, leaving the two guards with their throats cut.

Many of these atrocities could have been averted had the constables been more vigilant. Despite all the dangers attached to duty in these towers, it was not unusual, while on a surprise inspection, to find not one guard but both propped against the wall, fast asleep.

If the terrorists met opposition during an attack they normally kept up a barrage of fire over several minutes then withdrew as quickly as they had appeared. Two hours later they would be back again—this time directing their fury on the neighbouring tower. The psychological effect of these spasmodic raids was very powerful. The terrorists used this method to great advantage and in many instances it was their greatest weapon.

One of the settlements was situated at Pokok Sena, in Kedah. The village was constructed in the fork of two roads, giving it the perfect shape of a triangle, two sides of which offered no chance of terrorists approaching the fence without being spotted. The third side was a different proposition, as it backed on to secondary jungle, which, although dense, was a veritable rabbit warren of tracks and holes through the scrub bush and lallang (elephant grass).

It was in this setting that I prepared to lay an ambush in the hope that terrorists could be trapped in the act of picking up food planted for their use.

At first light, with my twenty-man squad, which included Osman and many of the others who had accompanied me on my first memorable sortie into the jungle, I set out from the station and made a wide detour of the village, to make camp beside a small stream about three miles from Pokok Sena. In groups of five we searched the surrounding countryside in an attempt to find a path which would take us, unobserved, to the more vulnerable side of the settlement. This proved a relatively simple task, as each of the four groups found paths offering a reasonable amount of cover.

When darkness fell, around 7 p.m., I left five men behind to guard the camp and took the rest of the squad to the point where all five paths converged. In a small clearing, which anyone following the paths was bound to cross, we set up our ambush spreading ourselves around the thicket. I issued orders to shoot on sight—the signal for this to be given when Osman opened fire with his Bren gun.

It was a clear moonlight night and as we lay in the tall lallang many sounds could be clearly heard, from the consumptive coughs of the older inhabitants of the settlement to the perpetual whirring and buzzing of the insects.

A herd of wild pigs came close, grunting and snorting as they tore up the ground in search of food. After a time they moved off, leaving us to listen to the high-pitched whine of the mosquitoes. Fortunately, before settling in our positions we had covered all exposed parts of our bodies with a potent insect repellent. Without it the situation would have been intolerable.

The long hours of night dragged past but no one came. Stiff and weary, we stole quietly away from our positions as the sky began to lighten and dawn crept over the horizon.

We had only travelled about two miles in the direction of the camp when the leading scout, about twenty yards in front of the file, stopped in his tracks and gave the signal to halt. One by one we dived into the lallang beside the path and flopped to the ground.

I heard voices coming from about thirty yards in front. One voice seemed to be doing all the talking when a second one broke in—this time speaking quickly and in a high-pitched tone. As I listened the voices grew louder and I could hear the rustling of the grass and vegetation as it brushed against clothing.

The leading man in the squad allowed the figures to pass him and when I judged by the sound of the voices that they were directly opposite I leaped out and grabbed the first man around the throat and threw him to the ground. Osman was right beside me and pounced on the second man, who was trailing a few yards behind his companion.

They struggled violently, but when the rest of the squad emerged from the lallang, with rifles levelled, and surrounded us, all resistance left them. Pinning my man face down on the path, I searched him, but my only find was a sheath knife. Osman's captive carried a similar weapon. They were both dressed alike—old khaki shirts and shorts which flapped around their knees—and appeared to be men in their early thirties. My capture was taller than his neighbour but thin as a rake.

My first questions were ignored, their only reaction being one of suspicion. But when I persisted the suspicion turned to insolence and they countered each question with a sarcastic grin. Osman knew the routine. He nudged a companion and I heard the click of a rifle bolt. Quickly I looked around and saw a constable looking along the sights of his rifle, the barrel pointing at the tall man's head. He saw it at almost the same time, because he was on his feet in a flash, babbling and shouting that he would tell me anything that I wanted to know. His companion was right behind him, yelling a similar entreaty.

I ordered the constable to lower his rifle and the two men poured out their story. They were Siamese and lived near Kuala Nerang about ten miles away. They had been on their way to look at some snares which they had set the previous day to catch wild pig. They were peaceful men and could not understand why the tuan and his men wished to be violent to them.

Their story over, I ordered their hands to be tied securely behind their backs and told them to lead us to the spot where the snares were set. We must have visited a dozen different places. On each occasion when nothing was found the men shook their heads and quickly led us in another direction. After an hour of fruitless tramping around I was certain they were lying. I said so. They vigorously denied the accusations, adding that the tuan must know how people came into the jungle and stole snares. This, to me, was certainly a new line of theft.

We marched back to our camp and tied them to a tree. A meal was prepared and one of the constables gave our two prisoners some rice to eat. They were now sullen and resentful—the bolder of the two kicking the dish, scattering the rice over the Malay's boots. A sharp knee in the groin from the policeman reminded the man of his manners.

When our meal was finished we headed for the main road to Kuala Nerang, and some distance away from Pokok Sena village I took two of the squad with me and walked back to the police post, leaving the remainder of the men and the two suspects hidden in the undergrowth. Telephoning to Alor Star, I requested transport to be sent to pick us up for the journey to Kuala Nerang.

I had not long to wait before two trucks appeared and we drove to the spot where my men lay hidden. They wasted no time in climbing aboard and fifteen minutes later we drove into the village where the two prisoners assured us they lived.

The tall man led us to a small atap hut where we were met by a thin-looking woman, whom I presumed was his wife, and a horde of children. We searched every corner, but nothing incriminating was found.

The second suspect was more evasive regarding the whereabouts of his hut, but after a good deal of shouting and rifle-prodding led us to a building on the outskirts of the village. Nothing was found in the hut and the man leered cheekily at me when he saw the search was over. The grin vanished from his face when I ordered the surrounding area to be combed and from time to time when I glanced over at him, as my men beat the undergrowth, I saw that he was sweating profusely and growing extremely tense. The reason for this was soon apparent.

A constable came on a quantity of cut lallang underneath some bushes about eighty feet from the hut. When this was cleared away we found a fifty-gallon drum, with a wooden lid, crammed with rice and foodstuffs. It was stocked to the brim and obviously ready for collection by the terrorists.

Owing to the isolated position of the hut it was possible for the terrorists to make the collection in daylight with reasonable safety. However, I thought morosely, there was little point in laying an ambush at the spot as we had been watched by a considerable number of the Chinese villagers during our search. There was every possibility that a message was already on its way to the terrorists warning them to stay clear as their cache of food had been unearthed.

While five of the squad took the two prisoners to Kuala Nerang police station, I ordered every hut and building to be searched. For most of the day we toiled in and out of the houses and hunted in the undergrowth on all sides of the village. But nothing more was found and the villagers maintained a tight-lipped silence.

They knew nothing of the activities of our two prisoners. What they did was their own affair was the general attitude adopted in reply to our questions. My greatest satisfaction at the end of the day was the knowledge that the terrorists knew we were suspicious of the Kuala Nerang villagers and would most likely give the place a wide berth.

At a special court the two Siamese were tried and convicted of harbouring food for supply to the terrorists. They were both sent to detention for several years.

Early in May I had to go to Nami police post with instructions to deploy my squad in searching for terrorist camps and traces of their movements. The post was situated about twelve miles south-east of Naka police station and had been attacked on over two dozen occasions. Fortunately for the occupants, these attacks had not been really serious efforts, consisting mainly of sporadic firing at the wooden buildings, by anything up to a dozen terrorists, from positions outside the perimeter barbed-wire fence. No attempt had been made to overrun the post.

It appeared to us that the camp was being used by terrorists for target practice to baptise new recruits in the art of shooting. Indeed, this fact had been mentioned several times in documents dealing with their training programme, which had been found by the security forces in hastily abandoned camps. But the fear was always present that sooner or later a full-scale attack would be launched and more policemen wantonly massacred.

There was a perfectly good path leading from Naka to Nami, but due to the number of houses scattered around on the outskirts of Naka, in which lived an assortment of Siamese and cross-bred Siamese-Malays, I decided to avoid it and cut through the secondary jungle, well clear of any habitation.

It was hard going and took us nearly three hours to cover four and a half miles until we struck back on to the main path to Nami.

From then on the going was simple, although we had to be cautious in case any terrorists might be lurking in the vicinity. Eventually we reached the post and when I had inspected it thoroughly I was entirely at a loss to understand why the Administration had decreed it should be built in such a useless position. It appeared to serve no useful purpose and stood forlorn and alone in the fork of two rivers, where the Sungai Sok joined the Sungai Muda. There was no human habitation nearby and consequently no cultivation, which would have aided the terrorists. There it was in the middle of nowhere, the tattered flag giving it some semblance of authority, just a few wooden huts with a dozen special constables guarding them, within a barbed-wire fence, through which entry could be made at any point using even the most blunt pair of wire-cutters.

The following morning I left the compound with five of

my squad and started a wide search of the outer perimeter, making careful note of all the vantage points from which the camp was clearly visible, thus giving the terrorists a clear line of fire. I came upon two positions about one hundred yards from the huts which had been used only a matter of days before, judging by the condition of a couple of spent .303 rounds, lying in the grass.

After the midday meal I set the men to work on strengthening the earthen parapets around the huts and deepening the slit trenches several yards in front of the buildings. When these tasks were completed I was fairly satisfied that we would be able to withstand any attempt to overrun us, provided the terrorists used a small force in their attack.

Before dusk I supervised the posting of the night guards and issued strict instructions that I was to be called should even the slightest sound outside the fence appear to be suspicious. I think that the Malays must have begrudged me my sleep on that first night as I lay on the bare boards of the floor in the central hut. I was shaken awake and blinded by the beam of a torch almost every half-hour. Each time I went outside and listened with the men to a variety of sounds, later identified as either small animals foraging for food or several wild pigs rooting up the ground alongside the fence, to an accompaniment of grunts and squeals. Eventually I gave up trying to sleep and spent the remaining hours of darkness huddled in one of the slit trenches.

For four nights the same vigil was repeated and all went smoothly. The conclusion that somehow or other the terrorists must have been alerted of the large number of policemen in the compound was beginning to form in my mind. However, I had time to spare and decided to continue for several more nights in order to be absolutely certain.

The next night, after darkness fell, I went with Osman and his mate, Ahmat, to one of the advanced trenches, several yards behind the wire. Prior to setting out for Nami and after a great deal of persuasion I had been able to obtain a second Bren gunner for the squad. As the gunner was down for the next stint of duty, I took his Bren with me. As we settled ourselves in the narrow trench Osman lined up on one of the positions found earlier in the week and I covered the the other.

Ahmat lay between us, a pile of spare Bren magazines in front of him. By now I was well used to the usual noises of the night, when the entire jungle seemed to come alive. Insects hummed, buzzed and whined, frogs called from the river banks with deep-throated bronchial croaks, pigs grunted, squealed and snorted as they tore up the croton undergrowth.

The pigs had been with us for around twenty minutes when I heard a coughing grunt coming from the trees about two hundred feet behind them. At once there was a fantastic scurrying and high-pitched squealing as they charged off into the bush.

Ahmat whispered: 'Tiger, tuan.'

I listened intently and picked up the sound of something moving through the lallang. The noise grew louder as it came closer, then stopped abruptly. Whatever had caused the commotion was standing still and, judging from where I had last heard the sounds of movement, within a few feet of the fence. I peered into the darkness, willing my eyes to see. For five minutes I stared ahead—no sound, no movement.

Then I saw the shape approach right up to the fence and stand still almost touching the wires. It was a tiger—and a magnificent specimen. I held my breath as I savoured the sight of the huge animal as he stood with his head held high, sniffing the air. He moved several feet to the left, then turned inwards once more, looking across to the huts. A sharp cough from one of the buildings cut through the air and the spell was broken. The tiger was gone with a flick of his mighty tail as he crashed into the lallang.

We settled down once more and before an hour had passed I heard more sounds of movement. This time they came from the general direction of the two vantage points covered by our Brens. It only took me five minutes to realise that this time it was no animal—the stealthy, slithering noises were being made by men as they dragged their bodies over the scrub and through the lallang.

Several men coughed from the interior of the huts and we took advantage of the noise to swiftly cock our Brens. The rustling noises continued and soon it was obvious that a number of men were making their way towards us. The sound split up and I was certain that within minutes we would be under fire.

It took the guerillas thirty minutes to start the attack. Several bursts of fire, almost simultaneously, came from the two points.

Osman and I immediately opened up and sprayed the firing positions until both magazines were emptied. Ahmat swiftly replaced them and our Brens spat out their fire once more. The terrorists replied with their rifles. Twice more we emptied our magazines. By this time the other special constables had joined in, firing their rifles in the general direction of the jungle. The din was terrific and the smoke from the Brens was thick around our heads.

The terrorists, although they must have been considerably surprised by the strength of our fire, kept up the attack for almost ten minutes. Due to the Brens they were unable to advance and we managed to keep them pinned down, gradually directing all our fire over a small area of jungle surrounding their two positions.

I sent Ahmat back to call a halt to the firing. When this ceased I heard groans coming from one of the positions and in the general direction of the other a man screamed in agony. A great deal of noise came from the undergrowth as it was torn apart and crushed as the remaining terrorists retreated. The screaming grew louder, then began to fade. I guessed that the wounded man was being dragged away by some of his companions.

I nudged Osman and we opened fire once more. Behind me the constables got to work with their rifles, but before long it was clear that the terrorists were not staying to fight it out. No more shots came from their positions and I ordered my men to cease fire. There was no point in following the fleeing marauders in the utter darkness. Our single torch, with its feeble light, would not have been of much use anyway.

At dawn I left the compound with ten men and crossed the scrub to the two positions. I saw clearly where seven or eight people had been lying, three at one spot and four or five at the other. A large number of spent .303 cases lay in the undergrowth and on top of the flattened lallang a mass of red ants fed greedily on a large pool of blood. Spots of blood marked the surface of the leaves at both positions. I was positive that several men must have been wounded and, judging by the cries of pain, one was severely injured.

It was a simple matter to follow their route of retreat. They had obviously departed in great haste, making no attempt to cover their tracks, taking their wounded or dead with them. The removal of the dead was standard practice, thus denying the security forces the knowledge of how successful they had been.

The trail led down to the river and then vanished. There was little choice in deciding which direction they must have taken. It was either upstream or down, as the Sungai Muda ran roughly from north-east to south-west. In either direction it flowed through secondary jungle and in some parts light bush and scrubland.

I chose the north-east and this led to the mountainous border with Thailand. I sent several men back to the post to collect rations and issue my orders for the remainder of the squad to split forces and search both banks of the river to the south-west.

We followed the stream, five on one bank and six on the other, for over four miles, but no traces of the terrorists could be found. Apart from some animal tracks and paths, no human had set foot in the area prior to our arrival. I abandoned the search and returned to the post, where we found that the other patrol had fared similarly, drawing a complete blank.

I felt sure that as the terrorists had no automatic fire when they attacked, their effort had been in the form of another training trip. Never before had their recruits received such a baptism of fire at Nami. They must have received a nasty shock, because the post was never attacked again and the guerillas moved elsewhere for target practice.

After spending three months based at Alor Star I was posted to Serdang in South Kedah, on June 7, as officer in charge of the Police District. This was the only part of Malaya I disliked. In the main the countryside was flat and uninteresting, with rubber trees covering a major part of the area.

Perhaps the chief reason for my dislike was the state of the accommodation provided for me. It was a house which had once belonged to a rubber plantation manager but had been abandoned because of its dilapidated condition. It stood among rubber trees and got very little sunshine. There were numerous large holes in the roof and I was forced to move my bed around depending on the velocity and direction of the wind. Shortly after I moved in the monsoon season began and hardly a night passed without my wakening up, drenched by the rain pouring through the roof. Mosquitoes kept up a constant invasion by day and night and after several weeks I wondered how the previous tenants had been able to preserve their sanity in such conditions. Although I was assured on many occasions that this was only to be temporary accommodation, while a new bungalow was being built, it was my home for my entire spell of duty in Serdang.

Ah Fong, my young Chinese orderly, appointed to cook and generally look after me, dropped frequent hints that he was finding it difficult to look after the house and keep it clean and tidy. I knew when Ah Fong protested that he must have a genuine grievance. He was with me for several years and our stay in Serdang was the only period during which he uttered one word of complaint. He went about his duties quietly and methodically, occasionally allowing a fleeting smile to pass over his boyish face when I joked with him or paid him a compliment. He was a faithful servant and, as he was only in his early twenties, proud of his position as the tuan's orderly, which gave him increased status over the servants of the junior police officers.

Several of the rubber estates were large and had European managers and assistants, who were most hospitable when I made my periodic visits with a small squad of constables. Most of the people on the European-owned plantations and tin mines led vulnerable lives and the assistant managers had the highest casualty rate of all. The huge combines who controlled these vast estates owe a great debt of gratitude to these men, who were mainly responsible for the flow of rubber out of Malaya when the Emergency was at its height.

The assistants, usually young men—some hardly out of their teens—bore the brunt of all the tasks in the most dangerous areas, as they inspected the trees and supervised the labour in the more remote parts of the estates where rubber came face to face with dense jungle.

In some cases they were provided with armoured cars or, more often than not, large American cars with armour plating on the sides and front windscreens. But these cars were useless when the monsoon torrents turned the dirt roads into tunnels of mud and the assistant managers were forced to carry out their duties on foot. Usually they were provided with a bodyguard of either one or two special constables, but the number of guards depended entirely on the generosity of the rubber company.

While these brave men faced danger daily, their bosses, the managers, sat snug and safe in their offices, surrounded by their own personal bodyguard—usually four or five special constables. It is only fair to say, though, that there were some brave and conscientious managers, who did their fair share of the dangerous field work, but the pro-

The Rolls-Royce in which Sir Henry Gurney, High Commissioner for Malaya, was assassinated (*Straits Times*)

This photograph, taken from the centre of the ambush position, shows policemen standing on the spot where Sir Henry Gurney's car was brought to a standstill (*Straits Times*)

After a ten-day jungle patrol Brodie returns to
civilisation

More formal uniform is needed for the Sultan
of Kedah's birthday

portion of these was small. An indication of just how small can be seen when one considers that approximately ninety-eight per cent of deaths and serious injury in the managerial category were all assistants.

Due to the rough and ready life they led, together with the constant threat of danger hanging over their heads, these young men certainly painted the town red whenever they were able to get some leave in either Kuala Lumpur or Penang. Their session of wine, women and song would be brief but thorough. The European snobs, of whom there were many in Malaya, tended to despise the wild antics of the assistant managers when they hit the town. But most knew my feelings—those who did not were swiftly informed —and did not dare make any criticism of their behaviour in my presence. What they said behind my back was their own affair.

In the Serdang district there were two main danger zones—the roads to Kulim and Selama. Ambushes were continually happening on the Selama highway and no planter's house escaped unscathed. There was not one plantation that had escaped the destruction of tractors and lorries and the burning of outhouses storing the raw rubber. At least four assistant managers were killed by the harrying bands of guerillas.

But the road to Kulim was the most notorious and earned itself the reputation of being the most dangerous road in north Malaya. Many police vehicles were shot up and a number of policemen killed including several Europeans. It was tailor-made for ambushes, twisting and turning through dozens of deep, rocky gorges and running through long stretches of dense jungle. Although the attacks by the terrorists were swift and numerous I combed the entire area, on a number of occasions, with small detachments of men, and only once saw anything of the elusive enemy.

I led patrols through the forest land and up the hilly ground, covered by thick jungle, and far out to the west

K

through the lallang and eight-foot-high ferns. I hunted the areas on every side of the roadway as far as the boundary of Serdang, with Kulim. I laid ambushes on paths and trails and spent torturous nights being chewed up by mosquitoes. I took our sole armoured vehicle, which was most effectively armour-plated around the driver's cabin and all round the sides and rear, but completely open at the top, making it a wonderful target for grenades lobbed from high ground, and patrolled the roads, at leisurely pace, inviting trouble. But none came.

The terrorists avoided detection and in all Malaya it must have been the craftiest and most wily, hand-picked to avoid capture, who were sent to this part of the country.

Only once did they slip up, but even then their run of luck held.

On one of our numerous patrols we rounded a corner on the road to find a lorry, blazing fiercely, on its side in the ditch. We pulled up and watched for any sign of movement in the lallang on the steep hillside. Twenty minutes went past with no signs of life until I saw the grass moving on top of the rise. The movement was repeated in several patches. I opened up with the Bren gun, giving my men the signal to fire, and poured a deluge of bullets into the places where the movements had been seen.

When the firing started I noticed further movement from several points on the side of the hill and more fire was directed in this region. The Communists had obviously been waiting for the arrival of security forces, attracted by the blaze. No doubt they had hoped that we would have left our vehicle immediately and walked straight into their ambush. However, it was now apparent that they suspected us of being a decoy vehicle, due to our prolonged wait, and were making off in the belief that other forces were flanking the hillside to trap them from behind.

Grabbing a Sten gun and leaving four men in the armoured truck, I went up the hill with the constables strung out behind me in pursuit. When we reached the top of the rise I saw there was a ridge of ground, about three feet high, from which a clear view could be obtained of the two vehicles on the roadway.

The positions where about ten men had been lying could be clearly seen in the flattened lallang, but the men had been well shielded from our bullets. No traces of blood could be found.

We hunted them for two hours, along a dried-up watercourse, through tunnels in the lallang and scrub trees and in and out of the dense thickets of bamboo. When we reached the edge of a rubber plantation I decided to give up, as a maze of paths, used daily and well trodden by the feet of the latex tappers, confronted us. Dispirited and frustrated that our prey had been able to escape, we made our way back to the road.

On entering Terap police station, to report the incident to the local policeman, I saw a corporal trying to placate a small Chinese man who was talking in excited tones and waving his thin scraggy arms around in the air. He was the driver of the lorry we had found burning and had walked the dry and dusty miles to Terap to report his loss.

He said he had been driving his empty vehicle back to a rubber estate when he was stopped by several armed men. They told him to get out of the cab and clear off. He did not argue and as he ran away the men pushed the lorry into the ditch and set fire to it.

I did not think, as I listened to the agitated man, that within several weeks, at almost the same point on this deadly stretch of roadway, I would run the gauntlet of terrorist fire described in Chapter 1, shortly before I left to take charge of the most northerly part of the Malay/Thailand frontier, at Padang Besar.

10

Opium—and a Look at the Future

APART from the many problems of frontier security at Padang Besar a great deal of my time was spent waging war against smugglers who operated in large numbers across the border.

The main culprits were women who would disgorge from the daily express from Bangkok, loaded with vegetables, dried fish, unwholesome-looking scraps of meat and a variety of oddments. With the money received for the sale of these items they bought cigarettes for re-sale in Thailand. Although this form of trading was banned under the Malayan Customs laws and the goods liable to be confiscated, this did not deter the women, who arrived in ever-increasing hordes each day. The vendors were mostly prostitutes, forced to give up their trade because they had grown too old or too ugly and scarred by a host of varieties of venereal disease. Occasionally a few young and exceptionally attractive prostitutes would alight from the train, but they still followed their original business and, for the most part, left the smuggling in the hands of the old crones.

The main item we searched for was opium. Many different ways were used to smuggle it into the country and I found it in small capsules concealed in meat, fish, the stalks of vegetables and, engaging the assistance of a female searcher, strapped to the bodies of many of the women. But the prostitutes and other passengers bringing the opium in on the trains were small fry. What we really wanted was to lay hands on the large consignments that somehow or other were getting through. I dropped the hint to several of the Siamese Customs officers that I would pay fifty dollars (approximately £6) if anyone could give me information leading to the discovery of a reasonable amount of opium.

To these men fifty dollars was considered to be a small fortune, as they did not even earn that amount in one month, being paid only half the wages received by their Malayan counterparts working at Padang Besar station.

One week later I was standing on the platform awaiting the arrival of the Bangkok express when one of my potential informers approached and casually slipped a grubby piece of paper into my hands, which were clasped behind my back. In the privacy of the Malayan Customs office I opened the note and immediately burst out laughing when I read the terse message scrawled in spidery handwriting: 'Investigate the anuses of fowls which are arriving this morning', it said. Although I thought it was a joke, I could not afford to take the risk of ignoring the information and with two Customs officers stepped out on the platform again.

The express arrived and there was a great deal of jostling and pushing as its many passengers poured out and dispersed in a variety of directions. The usual crowd of women got off, but there were no signs of any crates containing chickens. We went into a waiting-room, from which we could see the full length of the platform without being observed from the train. After about five minutes I saw two Chinese peering out from one of the carriages. One jumped down and looked up and down the platform, then signalled to his companion, obviously indicating that no policemen or Customs officials could be seen.

They then unloaded four crates amid much squawking from the fowls trapped inside. Another Chinese, whom I recognised as a local shopkeeper, walked quickly along the platform and was soon engaged in deep conversation with the two from the train.

Sending one of the Customs officers round the back of

the buildings to come in from the other end of the platform, I went out into the sunlight with the remaining officer and walked over to the three men. They were most polite when I told them I was taking the fowls to the Customs office for inspection and agreed to carry the crates for us. Even when I told them that I suspected they were smuggling the opium in the fowls they still maintained a general air of charm and wore expressions of pained innocence on their faces.

One of the Customs officers picked up a chicken and searched through its feathers, but replaced it in the crate, amongst its noisy companions, when nothing was found. I told him to have another look and this time to stick his finger into the bird to feel if anything was there. He looked at me, his mouth hanging open, quite sure that I had gone mad. However he obeyed, with a look of extreme distaste on his face. The other Customs officers followed suit, but after inspecting the first crate and finding no opium hidden in the two dozen chickens, I began to think that I had been tricked. I visualised the roars of laughter that would greet the tale of how I had been duped when it reached the ears of my friends in Alor Star.

The second crate produced nothing incriminating, as did the third. By now the room was littered with feathers and the Customs officers were growing extremely annoyed. When the fourth crate was opened I saw several birds squatting on the bottom, unable to get to their feet. When one was upended the reason for its discomfort was plain to see—the anus was stitched up. The stitches were cut and eight capsules fell on the floor.

The three Chinese shuffled their feet and tried to look surprised. I locked the door to prevent them from trying to escape and, putting the key in my pocket, got down to the business of inspecting the remainder of the chickens. Twenty fowls were similarly loaded and when the job was over one hundred and sixty capsules, amounting to a considerable quantity of opium, were stacked neatly on the table.

The three prisoners, with an escort of policemen and

Customs officers, together with the suffering poultry, were put aboard the next train south to Alor Star, where they later received stiff prison sentences for what was probably the most ingenious method of opium-smuggling ever to come my way.

Greatly satisfied with the capture, I declared wholesale war on the smugglers and within several weeks most of the vendors stopped coming to Padang Besar. This, however, had some shattering repercussions from another source. I received a letter from the Chief Customs Officer of the States of Kedah and Perlis, which shook me when I read the contents.

It said: 'I have received complaints that the steps which have been taken, since your arrival at Padang Besar, to bring petty smuggling under control have been so effective that a state of near famine has been reached by some of the more respectable members of the community, including subordinate members of our own Government and the Thailand Government.'

The letter concluded: 'Will you see whether it is possible to relax control a little without letting things get out of hand.'

After this I slackened off and within several days the vendors were back in large numbers. I allowed most of the vegetables and foodstuffs to get through, but, naturally, did not ease up any in the search for opium.

One worthwhile outcome of my complete clamp-down on the activities of the vendors was that I was receiving scraps of information passed on by the prostitutes, who were terrified that severe restrictions might be placed upon them again. Several spoke Malay, of which I now had a reasonable smattering, and when they spread themselves out at the rear of the platform, surrounded by a motley collection of fish, meat and vegetables, I was able to chat and joke with them as they haggled and argued with those who turned out to buy the wares.

One day one of the younger ones told me, in her halting

Malay, that there were some Chinese and Siamese orang jahats (villains) operating from a mining area near Kampong Telok in the hills on the Thailand side of the border. I thanked her and bent down and selected some vegetables. In payment I passed over a ten-dollar note for the fifty cents' worth received. She was delighted.

At this time the Press was full of news items concerning arms being smuggled across the border from Thailand to supply the terrorists in Malaya. When I thought about the Siamese woman's information as I tucked into one of Ah Fong's excellent beef curries in my bungalow that night, I reflected that a great deal of suspicion had been directed at the Chinese working in the tin mines at Kaki Bukit in Perlis, about twelve miles across the mountains from Kampong Telok. It was possible that a link existed.

The following morning, with five days' supply of rations, I set off with twenty men, along a track running through a wide expanse of lallang and up into the jungle-covered mountains. That night, after a hard day's slog, we made camp near a large bamboo thicket and I was initiated into the different uses of bamboo by Corporal Salleh. He showed me how water was to be found in different sections and also how to cook rice in a section of a stem.

For this purpose a section was cut below one joint and through the one higher up the stem. The rice was wrapped in the lead of a wild plantain, making a long cylinder, which was then fitted into the bamboo and pushed down the section. Some water was added and the bamboo was placed in an upright position in the glowing embers of the fire. There it was left to cook until the rice had swollen sufficiently to split the sides of the bamboo container. This was the signal that all was ready; the leaf with its contents was removed. The rice tasted more delicious, cooked in this manner, than any other way I have ever known and with our usual fare of curried pilchards and a small piece of dried fish was enough to put an edge on even the dullest of palates.

Corporal Salleh was a magnificent tracker—to him the floor of the jungle was a living book. To what appeared to me to be only a slight indent in the soil he would kneel down and after a quick inspection look up and say: 'Babi' (pig) or 'Rusa' (deer). He showed me the dangers of many of the jungle plants and warned me never to touch the fur of the green bamboos. This caused a painful irritation of the skin, and could be particularly troublesome between the fingers.

He said it had been known for a Malay woman, who wanted to dispose of her husband, to scrape the fur off the bamboo and mix it with his food. This normally caused severe stomach ulcers, resulting in a slow, agonising death for the unfortunate husband.

We spent another day cutting through the jungle and crossing a wide river which seemed to have as its bed a thick layer of black, stinking mud. On the morning of our third day out, as we drew near to Kampong Telok, I saw a large clump of palm trees ahead, with a screen of bushes and plants in front. Smoke rose lazily into the air from the centre of the palms.

Taking five men and leaving our packs with the rest of the squad, I slowly made my way towards the signs of life. We had not gone more than two hundred yards when Corporal Salleh signalled us to stop. He pointed in front. I went up to join him and through the undergrowth saw a small atap hut, standing on its own in a clearing between the trees. As we watched, an elderly Chinese appeared in the doorway and walked over to a group of plantains growing a few yards away. He picked off some of the green leaves near the top. Corporal Salleh whispered that the man might be using them to make opium packets. Clutching a bundle of leaves, the old man shuffled back across the clearing and disappeared into the hut.

We kept watch for some time, but when the old man did not reappear I decided to make a detour round the hut and investigate the village. There were plenty of tracks to choose from and signs that they were in constant use. Once more Corporal Salleh halted our file, saying that he had heard an elephant approaching. We hid in the long grass and within several minutes the great beast hove into view.

A Siamese mahout sat on the elephant's neck and a massive pair of crude panniers were slung over the animal's broad back. On the side next to me I saw that the pannier was loaded with full sacks. Corporal Salleh pointed out that they most likely contained tin ore, being transported from the nearby mines. When the elephant and his load were out of sight we crossed the dirt road and carried on to find ourselves within view of a number of houses, some roofed with rushes and others with pieces of corrugated iron.

For over two hours we lay in the undergrowth watching the womenfolk moving around and talking, while the children laughed and chased each other as they played in and out of the houses. Leaving Corporal Salleh and a couple of men to keep watch, I went back to the clearing where I had seen the old man.

Once more I watched him leave the hut and pick some of the young leaves from the wild plantains. Far away on the left I heard the faint sound of voices and I saw the old man stop work and look in their direction. A low voice called from the fringe of the brush and the old Chinese answered. Four men entered the clearing—three appeared to be Malays and carried single-barrelled shotguns, while the fourth was a middle-aged Chinese. Soon the two Chinese were talking earnestly to each other while the other three men lit cigarettes and sat down beside the hut.

Our hiding place was too far away to be able to overhear the conversation and after ten minutes the visiting Chinese left the old man and crossed over to speak to the Malays. He was gesticulating all the time and I saw him point to the sun, which was now sinking low, then indicate towards the hut.

The three men got up and went to a raised platform, covered by an atap roof, and laid out some food. One lit a fire. We retreated from our hiding place and went back to join Corporal Salleh. As we sat by our camp-fire I told him of what I had seen and he confirmed my growing suspicions. The middle-aged Chinese was an opium-buyer, while the three Malays were his bodyguard. Most likely they intended to return to Kaki Bukit in the morning, carrying a fresh consignment.

At first light we crossed the river and on the edge of a swamp set up an ambush on a track where fresh footprints were visible heading in the direction of the Siamese village. Time passed slowly, and the mosquitoes, from the muddy region of the swamp, fell on us in droves. A troop of long-tailed monkeys, chattering and screeching, passed overhead. Fortunately they did not see us crouching in the under-growth. If they had, their calls of alarm would have been unmistakable to the men, whom we hoped were making their way towards us.

Corporal Salleh touched my arm and pointed along the track. The warning was passed along. I could not hear anything and it was nearly a minute before I picked up the sound of feet padding towards us. Through a break in the scrub I saw four men approaching, walking in single file.

They began to pass by and when all were in the centre of the ambush area we leaped to our feet and confronted them. They were completely taken aback and before the Malays had a chance to fire their shotguns we had a variety of weapons jammed against their backs and stomachs. The last thing they had expected was to be pounced upon in a wild and remote area by a bunch of men in dirty jungle green and a fearsome-looking European with a tattered hat on his head and a three days' growth of beard on his face.

The three shotguns were seized and all three men were relieved of the wicked-looking sheath knives carried at their belts. The Chinese was unarmed and looked dispirited that his fine bodyguard had let him down and given in without even so much as a small struggle.

Tying their arms behind their backs, I opened their packs. Apart from some items of food and ammunition, the bags were entirely filled with small packages of opium wrapped in plantain leaves. The opium was a brown resinous substance and it was difficult to believe that this, when it reached the back-street dens and hovels of cities such as Singapore, Hong Kong and Tokyo, could be the cause of so much human misery.

The four looked a little more cheerful when I informed them that we were policemen; they obviously suspected us of being a gang of bandits who would relieve them of their cargo, then cut their throats. The Chinese man's identity card showed that he lived in Kangar, Perlis, but the Malays had no documents on them and would not say where they lived. They protested that they had no idea what the Chinese man intended to do with the opium, as they only acted as his bodyguard to and from Thailand. For this task they received ten dollars each. The Chinese remained silent and refused to volunteer any information.

I did not want to show face in Kaki Bukit, where I was sure all the men would be well known, and decided instead to head for a railway halt at Titi Tinggi, about nine miles to the south-east, where it was possible to stop a train in the middle of the jungle. When the train came along it halted when signalled to do so, but the driver was suspicious as he looked down from the cabin of his mighty locomotive. It took quite a long conversation by Corporal Salleh to convince him that we were in fact police and not terrorists, as he had feared because of our appearance.

Keeping six men with me I sent Corporal Salleh on to Padang Besar with the remainder of the squad, with orders to send back our railway jeep. He was also told to get the inspector to contact Kangar police station and have him send police transport to meet us at Bukit Ketri, a small kampong at the side of the railway line.

In about thirty minutes the railway jeep arrived and, with our four prisoners, we crammed ourselves in the interior and set off to rendezvous with our transport. The four men were deposited at Kangar and with some Customs officers I went to the shop owned by the Chinese man. He had either been in the process of renewing his stock when we caught him, or was careful never to keep any opium about the premises, because a thorough search failed to reveal anything remotely incriminating.

When our haul from the ambush was tallied there were more than four hundred packages, which would, no doubt, have been sold for around ten dollars each. Although the tip-off from the prostitute had not produced any terrorists, at least one more opium-dealer was out of business, making it just that little bit more difficult for the men behind this evil trade to operate.

Although we were not to realise it at the time, the news that a band of terrorists had assassinated the High Commissioner, Sir Henry Gurney, was to indicate the turning-point of the Emergency. The cruel and senseless killing of a man who, above all else, loved Malaya and its people was to spell disaster for the Communists. Although, undoubtedly, a first-class civilian administrator, Sir Henry was a kind and gentle man. He seemed unable to understand that only drastic, and in many cases ruthless, action could finally crush the terrorists.

He died on October 6, 1951, at 1 p.m. while travelling with his wife, Mr. D. J. Staples, his twenty-nine-year-old private secretary, and a police escort, from Kuala Lumpur to the mountain resort of Fraser's Hill, about seventy miles north of the Federation's capital. The party, travelling in two cars, the first containing seven constables, was ambushed on the Pahang-Selangor border, fifty-two miles from Kuala Lumpur.

The guerillas, later believed to have numbered more than forty, hiding in a thicket of bamboo, high above the narrow road, raked the small convoy with automatic fire. After all the police officers in the first car were wounded, the terrorists turned their attention on the large gleaming

Rolls-Royce used by the High Commissioner. As the first of the bursts, which were to strike the car thirty-five times, tore through the bodywork and punched holes in the windscreen Sir Henry jumped into the road in an attempt to draw the fire away from his wife.

His action was successful, although within seconds his body lay sprawled on the grass at the edge of the road as the guerillas concentrated their full fire power on him. He was struck several times and must have died almost immediately.

When the High Commissioner fell to the ground the terrorists ceased their attack and swiftly withdrew into the dense mountain jungle. Lady Gurney was unharmed and Mr. Staples escaped with slight injuries. The driver of the car was severely wounded in the head.

Because of the isolated position it took nearly an hour before the alarm was raised and although the entire area was combed by British and Gurkha troops and blasted by the Royal Air Force, no trace of the assassins could be found. On the following day an area of dense jungle, suspected of being the probable hide-out of the terrorist band, was heavily bombed for several hours by British and Australian aircraft.

There was every reason to suspect that the Communists had been tipped off about the High Commissioner's intention to visit Fraser's Hill. Only ten minutes before Sir Henry's Rolls-Royce reached the ambush point a car containing the Flag Officer, Rear-Admiral H. W. Faulkner, and his wife, with a naval driver in uniform, passed by unmolested.

There was a great deal of speculation in the weeks following the assassination as to who would be appointed head of the Administration and in January 1952 events began to move swiftly. On the 14th, Mr. W. N. Gray, the Federation's Police Commissioner, and Sir William Jenkin, the Director of Intelligence, tendered their resignations, following a visit to Malaya by Mr. Oliver Lyttelton, the Colonial Secretary. An official announcement, made from London, pointed out: 'There is no connection between the two resignations.'

The next day Mr. Lyttelton announced the appointment of fifty-three-year-old General Sir Gerald Templer as High Commissioner for Malaya and added that General Templer, in addition to the normal civil duties of his office, would direct all military and police operations and would be charged with full and direct responsibility for them. The statement added that it was also intended to appoint a Deputy High Commissioner on the civil side.

Three days later the British Government asked the Corporation of the City of London to grant their Commissioner, Colonel Arthur Edward Young, twelve months' leave of absence to carry out the reorganisation of the Malayan Police. On January 24 the request was granted.

When General Templer arrived in Malaya he set to work with a vengeance on a total reappraisal of the civil and military sides of the Administration. All the dead wood was swiftly and ruthlessly removed from the Administrative tree—some to be thrown away for good, some relegated to the lower branches.

More troops were brought into the country, better armoured vehicles provided, the Air Force strengthened and, when the combined forces began full operations, a tighter clamp was placed on all towns and villages.

Snap road blocks were set up, manned by British and Commonwealth troops working in conjunction with Malay policemen. Villages were thoroughly searched on the slightest suspicion, and curfews, up to twenty-two hours a day, enforced on villages known to be actively supporting the terrorists. Gradually, this new show of power began to have the desired effect and as kills and surrenders of terrorists started to increase, so the number of casualties among the security forces went down.

Colonel Young was not long in rejuvenating the police force. When he came to Malaya he found a force that, even within European ranks, contained many different factions.

The first and main body, occupying all the most senior administrative posts, belonged to the old Malayan Police group. The next in line had come from India when it was granted its independence. Both these categories belonged to the same school of thought, where the most outstanding qualification was primarily the sort of tie one wore. First and foremost they were administrators and, apart from one or two exceptions, not policemen.

The third category was the Palestine influx, transferred to Malaya after that country was partitioned, while the fourth and final group was composed of policemen who had been recruited from Britain. The latter two categories were all experienced policemen, with knowledge gained in various branches of the police service, but as few had the opportunity of having attended the recognised schools, were most definitely classed as inferior beings. Colonel Young conducted a thorough and searching study of the running of the force and in a comprehensive report which covered all aspects of police work, summed it up in two words: 'Organised disorganisation.'

Thanks to Colonel Young, with the full backing of General Templer, we soon found ourselves receiving better weapons and vehicles, which in the long run made our task a great deal easier. The special constables were particularly delighted when they received their first consignment of new Mk. V rifles as well as more Brens, Stens and .300 American carbines, which proved to be most effective for fast jungle-shooting.

It was now June 1952 and I was well settled in Padang Besar when a signal came from Alor Star instructing me to report back, to take up the post of Food Control Officer for the States of Kedah and Perlis. At first I thought I would find myself back behind a desk, but a quick wireless message to headquarters informed me that the job would require a considerable amount of field work as the Administration had introduced new regulations and wished much stricter control observed over the entire area. I was to work in unison with Ray Gibson, a civil servant attached to the Secretariat.

It saddened me to leave the fine bunch of Malays who had stood by me through thick and thin during our many sorties into the jungle and taught me a great deal about the people and the countryside. Two goats were killed that night and a huge feast prepared, washed down by considerable quantities of potent, chemical Malayan beer.

Next morning I stepped aboard the train for Alor Star and took my seat opposite a saffron-robed Buddhist priest and his accompanying small boy. As these priests are not allowed to touch worldly goods, each one, when leaving the temple, takes a boy with him who can accept money and any offerings on behalf of his master.

The train had just started to gather speed on a steep downhill gradient when the priest leaned forward and asked me, in perfect English, if I would mind if he looked at my hands.

'I have been studying you and believe I can foretell some of your future, tuan. If you will allow . . .'

He caught hold of my hands, turned them palms downwards and ran his slim fingers over the backs. I did not speak, but was highly sceptical of the whole business.

He placed my hands in my lap and settled himself in his seat. The boy looked up at him as if seeking inspiration from the face, partly hidden in the saffron hood. For several minutes the priest sat and stared as the train rocked and swayed over a bumpy section of the track.

'It will be many years, tuan,' he said at last, 'but you will marry and have two children, a boy and a girl. Before this, however, you will be involved in two serious accidents, but do not fear, you will survive them and have no lasting injuries. When you die it will be at a ripe old age.'

I smiled as politely as I could. I was still an unbeliever.

I put my hand in my pocket for some money to give to the boy, but the priest held up his hand.

'No, tuan, not yet . . . I am not quite finished. You see, I

L

have to say that you are proceeding on a journey to fresh surroundings. When you get there you will have a new job.'

I sat bolt upright as the full meaning of his words struck me. The look of amazement on my face must have been plain to see, judging by the quiet smile on the serene face of the priest and the look of wonder in the clear blue eyes of the boy who sat at his side.

Muttering my thanks, I handed a five-dollar note to the boy and went in search of the restaurant car. For once in my life I really felt I needed a drink.

I I

When the Laughter Changed to Fear

I T W A S was when I recovered consciousness and found myself jammed behind the steering wheel of my car, with smelly canal water lapping around the middle of my chest, that I realised the first of the Buddhist priest's prophecies had come true.

I had been back in Alor Star for almost four months when I got the opportunity of spending a weekend at a rest house on the 3,978 ft. summit of Gunong Jerai. Alistair Scott, the private secretary to the British Adviser in Kedah, George Dack, a Special Branch officer, and his wife Jean also intended to be present and went on ahead on the Friday afternoon. As arranged, I set off in my Austin A.40 early on the Saturday morning.

Part of the journey took me through great stretches of paddy plains, which gave the area the tag of Malaya's rice bowl, and for about twenty miles the road ran directly alongside a canal. Anxious to waste no time in joining the others, I kept my foot well down on the accelerator. The road was fairly busy, with cars and military vehicles travelling in both directions. On a long straight stretch I noticed a lorry several hundred yards ahead, moving slowly and keeping well in to the grass verge.

As I drew closer the reason for its snail-like progress became obvious. The vehicle was in a shocking state of repair, the tailboard hung at an angle and the sides were broken and bent. I sounded my horn and pulled out to pass.

The Chinese driver, who must have been dreaming in a world of his own, was brought smartly back to reality by the raucous blast of the horn and swung his ancient lorry out into the middle of the road, completely blocking my path.

I stood on the brakes, but by this time was too close. All I could do was wrench the steering wheel over and swerve. As the bank sloped sharply away from the highway down to the canal, I tried to pass with the two nearside wheels on the road and the offside ones on the slope. The car bucked and bounced as it hit the grass and I was almost convinced I had made it when the lorry-driver suddenly pulled his vehicle back to the nearside. The tail swung round and crashed against the side of the car. As I lost consciousness in a blinding flash of light I saw the sky turn a complete circle, then the grass, then the sky again, then water . . . and utter blackness. Somersaulting three times, the car came to rest on its wheels, on the canal bed.

When I came round my head was numb, and cold, dirty water oozed and sucked around my chest. I tried to move, but the steering wheel held me tight. One side of the car was smashed in, trapping me in a narrow space. The steering column had bent with the severe impact and the wheel pressed against my chest like some giant hand attempting to restrain me.

A crowd of Malays slid and slithered down the steep bank and splashed through the canal towards me. Two hauled on the door, but it refused to budge, the bodywork being knocked out of shape at the central pillar. The windscreen, as well as the door windows, were completely shattered. After breaking off the remaining pieces of glass, some of the smaller ones leaned into the car and tried to push the door out. It stayed firm. They then turned their attention on the steering wheel, but had little better luck in this direction.

The Malays offered words of encouragement to me and shouted instructions at each other as they clambered all over the car, doing their best to free me. I began to feel sick and put my hand up to my head, which seemed numb and remote from the rest of my body. The top felt smooth and sticky. I explored the back and my hand closed over a hairy flap lying against my neck. To my horror, I realised I had been almost completely scalped by the top of the windscreen when my head had exploded against it on the first impact.

The irregular sound of a two-stroke motor-cycle came near and two of the Malays ran up the slope. Unable to see up on to the road, I listened to the engine stop; then European women's voices asking the Malays what had happened. The voices drew near and as I turned my head, at the sound of splashing, saw Helen Coleman, wife of the Agricultural Adviser, and her sister Joyce, wading towards the car. I lifted my left hand out of the water to raise it in a greeting and saw, for the first time, the blood pumping out from a deep wound in the wrist. Helen gasped when she saw it and I felt my stomach turn when I looked at the long sliver of glass, sharp as a razor's edge, embedded in the artery. Whipping off her scarf Helen applied a tourniquet above the wound and sent her sister to stop the first lorry that came along and attempt to obtain a chain or rope, which could be fixed to the door of the car to wrench it off.

We had not long to wait and with the aid of a lorry and a stout rope the door was pulled off. The steering wheel was next and at last I was free. Gently, three Malays helped me out of the car and supported me across the canal and up the slope. Joyce, who was standing at the edge of the road, turned to speak to me and promptly fainted. No one could blame her. I looked hideous, with the top of my head covered in blood and raw flesh, my clothing bloodstained and soaked in muddy water. To add a macabre effect to an already horrific scene, several buffalo leeches, filled to capacity with the blood they had managed to suck, clung to my face, neck and arms.

An ambulance arrived and I was rushed to Alor Star Hospital, leaving Helen and her sister to continue on their journey to Penang.

In the cool hospital theatre I was cleaned up, X-rayed, my wounds stitched and given a large blood transfusion. Ironically the Indian doctor who carried out the transfusion had been on duty the previous day when I had gone to the hospital in answer to a call for donors to give blood for a young Chinese boy, severely stabbed in a brawl at Kuala Nerang.

I stayed in hospital for several days and when released took things easy for a time. The healing completed on my scalp, the stitches were removed. At two points on the top of my head I could feel solid bumps. For days I kept scratching at them until the skin was broken over one. I was then able to feel a hard substance. I mentioned my com-complaint to Jimmie Ferguson, the surgeon at Kedah Hospital, when I met him in the club that night. He only needed a few seconds to make his diagnosis.

With a laugh he told me: 'No wonder you're feeling a bump . . . you've got half the windscreen sewn into your scalp.' It was rather an overstatement, but his nimble fingers did pull two small cubes of glass from my head.

When the post of officer in charge of the Jitra Police District, in the north of Kedah, became vacant, I asked for it. My request was granted and on November 4, 1952, I moved north again to live in a modern bungalow, well removed from the village of Jitra and situated on the main Thailand to Singapore highway. As well as directing operations from the headquarters in Jitra I was also responsible for five sub-stations scattered over a wide region. One of these was situated at Sanglan, a fishing village on the coast, and in a wide belt of paddy lands a notorious band of Malays ruled over the terror-stricken local population.

Their chief victims were peasant farmers—owners of small patches of land. Their normal practice was to approach the farmer and demand payment of a sum of money. If he refused they would steal his buffalo and sell it themselves. To a paddy farmer a buffalo is as necessary as a well-trained dog is to a shepherd. In great fear of fierce reprisals the terrified farmer would not go near the police. Gradually, over a period of months, the gang had reduced the normally happy and carefree rice-growing community to a dejected, embittered body of men and women.

No matter how much I questioned the farmers they would not talk. Eventually a few did give some fairly harmless information, but refused point-blank either to press charges or to give evidence in court. The local police did their best to cope and after an intensive few days of investigation, and drawing a blank all the way, I returned to Jitra.

Almost one week later an excited constable hammered on the door of my bungalow with the message that ten members of the gang had come into Jitra and entered the town's one and only cinema. They had made no attempt to conceal large sheath knives, slung on their belts, and the leader had been carrying a small axe.

At the headquarters I mustered all the policemen who were on duty or resting, if their homes were near enough to the station. In fifteen minutes over thirty policemen had crowded into the main hall and I told them of the gang's arrival in town. When all were armed and well supplied with ammunition we went out into the street. The lights were dim and as we marched down the pavement inquisitive faces peered out from doorways and the bar windows as the sound of tramping feet echoed among the buildings.

The cinema stood just off the main street, near the outskirts of the town, and as we neared it a roar of laughter, accompanied by the sound of bells clanging and drums beating, swept out into the night. I was thankful for the row—it was such a noisy film that any sounds of our approach would be muffled.

Three policemen, all armed with rifles, were placed at each of the exits. They were given orders to shoot should any of the gang attack them. With ten men I entered the cinema, giving the cashier—a thin-faced Indian—a nasty shock as he dozed behind the window of his tiny cubicle. We went to the swing doors leading into the theatre. I opened one a few inches and looked through the crack. On the screen a man in Malay costume banged furiously on a large drum while several women danced round in the middle of a hall, which, judging by the elaborate setting, appeared to be a palace. A quick glance showed me that almost all the seats were taken, with men, women and children packed tightly together on the hard, wooden benches.

If I attempted to take the gang in the crowded cinema it was possible that many innocent people could find themselves caught up in a bloody battle. If I waited until the performance was over the gang were almost certain to escape, by hiding themselves in the centre of the vast crowd pouring out into the street. I went back to the door, lit a cigarette and pondered over my problem. The policemen waited. I only needed a few puffs before my mind was made up.

I sent one constable upstairs to the projection room to stop the film and switch on the lights. With the remaining nine men I moved towards the swing doors. One by one we entered the theatre and spread ourselves around the back and at the top of the aisles, in the centre and at each side.

Several people sitting near the door switched their attention from the activities on the screen to stare at us, as we took up our positions. I prayed that my man upstairs would not be too long in getting the lights on, otherwise it would not take many minutes for the whisper that the police were inside to spread through the audience. I could see the message being passed along and more heads were turned and necks craned in an attempt to see us.

With a deep, groaning noise the film came to a stop and the lights came on. The constables gripped their rifles and I felt the comforting weight of the .38 automatic in my right hand. The roar of disapproval that had come from the startled audience, who obviously thought the film had broken down, soon died to a hush when they saw the grim-faced constables looking around the theatre in an effort to spot the gang members.

They were not long in getting to their feet. They had been sitting only several rows from the front and as they rose I saw several reach for their knives. The leader unbuckled the axe from his belt. Some women, sitting behind them, screamed and tried to push their way out into the aisles. A wave of panic swept over the audience and benches were pushed backwards as many got to their feet. I shouted at them to sit down so that we could arrest the men. Some obeyed, while others shouted and pushed those in front.

The gang split up and went to the two exit doors on either side of the screen. The doors burst open and with harsh words of command the constables ordered the men to throw their weapons on the floor. Rifle bolts clicked and four gang members obeyed without a murmur. The others turned and advanced up the theatre towards us.

I shouted that we would shoot to kill if they came any closer and did not give in peacefully. A constable repeated my warning in Malay. Other exit doors opened and the appearance of more policemen added extra weight to my threat. Only the leader, a broad-shouldered man with a bullet-like head and pock-marked face, took no notice.

He snarled his contempt at the others who raised their hands in surrender and lunged up the centre aisle towards me. To have shot him would almost certainly have meant death or severe injury to at least one of the terrified audience. I had only seconds to make my decision—in fact everything happened so quickly that I was not conscious of even attempting to reach a decision of whether or not to shoot. With a cry of anger the constable standing next to me threw himself into mid-air and brought the butt of his rifle crashing into the gang leader's face. There was a sound of bones breaking as the heavy wood shattered his nose and broke most of his teeth. The axe dropped on the floor and its owner collapsed, prostrate, beside it.

All was quiet for several seconds and then, as children will do when watching a film where the 'goodies' defeat the 'baddies', the audience cheered.

We took the nine thugs out into the street and marched them to the station. All thoughts of watching a comedy forgotten, the audience swarmed out and followed us all the way to headquarters. The leader, carried by two constables, had his nose attended to by a doctor and several hours later I charged them all with possessing offensive weapons. The small axe, mounted on a slender pliable shaft, had an edge so sharp that it was possible to shave the hair off the back of my hand.

Next morning they made their court appearance and were remanded in custody. I drove to Sanglan and visited several of the paddy farmers whom I knew had been victimised. When they were assured that the gang were safely behind bars they agreed to press charges and promised to come forward to give evidence.

Further charges were made against the men and when the case had its final court hearing the paddy farmers kept their pledge. The evidence of five of them was sufficient to convince the judge that the charges had been proven. All ten thugs were given long terms of imprisonment.

While at Jitra I took an active part in athletics, both in the police team and the team representing the State. Many of the Malay policemen developed an interest in hammer throwing and putting the shot and when the various sports days came round there was great rivalry among them as they showed their prowess. They were enthusiastic pupils and coaching them was one of the most pleasant and relaxing tasks I ever undertook. Their joy knew no bounds on the day of the police sports when they triumphed over all the other teams and won half the trophies. I had some tough opposition in the shot and discus competitions myself, but, after a good struggle, managed to come out on top.

Because of the intense heat and humidity I found both the training and competition more arduous than I had ever done in Britain. It only needed a couple of practice throws with the hammer to work up a fine lather of sweat. But the exercise was good for us and the element of competition among the policemen brought a greater sense of team spirit which, in the long run, paid dividends during long jungle patrols.

At my bungalow I accumulated a vast number of pets which included a pelandok, or mouse deer, an otter, four different species of monkeys and six doves.

Dickie, the gibbon monkey, had the complete run of the house and was continually getting in Ah Fong's way, resulting in him spending much of his time chasing around and cleaning up after the elusive little beast. He got up to all sorts of mischief, including opening bags of flour and throwing the contents round the rooms and chewing letters if they were left lying in some spot within his reach. One day, after some particularly mischievous play, he raced out of the house, climbed a pole at the rear and was electrocuted by the cables fixed to the top.

The otter was perhaps the most affectionate of all. I had a spacious pen made for him and placed in it a huge zinc bath, full of water, for him to play in. Within a few days of obtaining him he had learned to trust me completely and, before long, whenever I returned home from Jitra I would hear his incessant whistling as he tried to attract my attention. I would go to his pen and open the door. Gambolling and jumping around my feet, he would keep up his whistling until I picked him up. With an overwhelming display of affection he would rub his silky muzzle, with the long, slender whiskers, against my face. His favourite game was running up one of my legs, when I was seated on the ground, around my neck and back down my other leg again. When he had enough he just curled up and went to sleep in my lap. When I went walking he would follow at my heel, like a well trained dog, and never seemed to mind how far the distance. Sadly, he too, came to an unfortunate end.

Going to his pen one morning, as I always tried to do

before driving to headquarters, I found him lying on his side, his face and eyes puffed up and hideously swollen. He was quite dead. The vet told me later that he had died from the bite of a cobra.

The pelandok was brought to the bungalow by a Malay hunter. He explained that he had stumbled over the tiny creature as it lay sleeping in a thicket. It had a long drooping nose, large brown eyes, appealing enough to touch even the hardest of hearts, a small sleek body and legs no thicker than a standard lead pencil. To these were attached dainty cloven hooves. Friends assured me that it was impossible to keep such a young beast in captivity, but they were to be proved wrong. In less than two weeks it was accepting food and titbits from my hand and when released from its cage showed no signs of wishing to leave, but played in and out of the house and on the long verandah.

The long-tailed and pigtailed monkeys were great acrobats, the latter being a clever individual who never tired of showing his party piece—a backwards somersault. In comparison the fruit monkey's movements, by day, were slower and more deliberate. When darkness fell his whole outlook on life changed. His sluggishness left him and he was able to show a remarkable turn of speed. He was small, with a golden-brown coat and huge lustrous eyes, and enjoyed climbing into the pockets of my jacket or, more usually, sitting in the breast pocket of my shirt, his tiny head peering over the edge.

My collection of animals and birds never failed to amuse those who paid a visit to the bungalow. In addition to the fun they gave, they were able to provide me with wonderful opportunities of studying at close hand some of the wild life with which Malaya abounds.

The first real opportunity of any big-game hunting came to me when a Malay from a remote kampong, situated on the banks of the Sungai Perik, walked into my office and reported that a tigress had killed a half-grown water buffalo belonging to one of the villagers. The beast had been attacked as it grazed in a clearing near the kampong and beside the dense jungle which stretched far up the mountains behind the river. Part of the carcase had been eaten, but as much remained it was thought that the tigress would return to finish her meal. The water buffaloes were precious to the villagers, depending on them for the heavy cultivation work. If the tigress had found it easy to kill one there was no doubt that it would be back for more.

I told the man to leave the carcase where it lay and to find a suitable spot where I could sit during the night and await the beast's return. Late in the afternoon I drove to the kampong, ending up by walking the remainder of the journey as no road had been built to connect it with the main highway. I found the buffalo lying in the open and although near dense, low scrub there was not a reasonable-sized tree around within easy shooting range. Vast thickets of bamboo grew at the back of the kampong and I sent several of the villagers to cut lengths, of varying sizes, from them. Each piece was split and one end pointed.

The pieces of bamboo were driven into the ground to form three circles of different heights, from about two to five feet. The stakes were placed at an angle of approximately forty-five degrees pointing outwards and, as each was hammered into the ground, it was sharpened to a needle point. Should the tigress turn up and, in the event of being wounded, attack the position, I would get some measure of protection as it impaled itself on the spikes. The circle was finally draped with brushwood and when the job was finished looked, for all the world, like a clump of bushes.

Suitably fortified by a huge meal of rice and dried fish, prepared by the wife of one of the villagers, I returned to my hide-out, with a flask of coffee, shortly after 6 p.m., just as the first signs of darkness approached. A strong breeze blew towards me from the direction of the jungle and as the moon rose it bathed the clearing in its cold, gentle light. I was able to see every detail of the carcase and some distance beyond it to the dark edges of the jungle. I made myself comfortable in my cramped quarters and laid the Browning automatic shotgun, loaded with cartridges and packed with buck shot, across my knees. One cartridge was in the breech and four in the magazine. All five shots could be blasted off as fast as the trigger could be pulled. Beside me lay my Sten gun, to be used in the event of dire emergency.

No mosquitoes bothered me—scared off by the strong insect repellent with which I had liberally covered myself—and there were few sounds apart from the rustling of the leaves from the jungle trees as the wind forced its way through the foliage. Now and again a bird squawked and on several occasions the monotonous tock-tock call of a nightjar rose above the other sounds and drifted away on the wind. I kept my eyes firmly fixed on the carcase but soon found that I was seeing all sorts of movement, which proved to be purely imaginary. When I changed my methods and looked at the dead buffalo for short periods, then glanced away elsewhere, then back again, I found I was no longer troubled.

A loud swishing sound made me sit up and tighten my grip on the shotgun but it was a false alarm. I looked up and saw a huge flock of flying foxes passing overhead. Belonging to the bat family and living solely on various kinds of fruits, these flying foxes, in Malaya, had a wing span of about two feet, with their heads resembling those of tiny foxes. I looked at my watch. It was 8.30 p.m., only two and a half hours since I had entered the hide-out. It had seemed like an age.

I had barely lowered my arm again when I heard the rustle of the coarse grass. I looked towards the carcase and saw the tigress. It stood, almost touching the body of the buffalo, with its great head turning slowly from side to side as it sniffed the air and gazed around the clearing. I held my breath as I saw it looked directly at my hide-out and for several seconds was afraid it had picked up my scent. Although it could not see me, the intensity of its stare made my flesh crawl. With a grunt it sank to the ground and lay alongside the carcase. I heard the rasp of its tongue as its mouth closed over a piece of flesh.

Silently, I raised the butt of the shotgun until it was at eye level and aimed at a spot just under the beast's left ear. For a split second I checked my bearing then gently squeezed the trigger. The noise of the shot cracked through the clearing and the tigress sprang into the air. Quickly, I snapped the second shot behind its shoulder as the beast struck the ground again.

The echoes of the shots died away and in the distance I heard the voices of the villagers as they ran towards the clearing. I remained in the hide-out for several minutes, but the beast did not move from the grotesque position it had adopted, half-slumped over the body of its victim of the previous night.

Re-loading the shotgun, I crawled out and stepped cautiously towards it. I had no need to worry. The animal had been killed with the first shot—its dramatic leap into the air the result of a convulsion when the heavy shot penetrated the brain. By now a crowd of excited villagers had burst into the clearing, chattering and laughing as they contemptuously kicked the body of the slain tigress.

The headman took my arm and invited me to his hut for tea, to celebrate the occasion. As I sat sipping the hot brew and munching through the sweet cakes prepared by his wife, I mentioned that I would like to remove the skin and have it cured. The headman shook his head. There would not be much point to this, he said, because there was no taxidermist anywhere in north Malaya. Nevertheless, I decided to have a go, with the idea of having the curing job done in Kuala Lumpur.

When I got back to the clearing there was no need to bother. The villagers were still there, shouting and clapping each other on the back. They had done a first-class job of mutilating the body. The whiskers had been cut off, the skin slashed and one man was in the act of removing the last of the claws. He was generous and gave me two, which

I later mounted and presented to friends. I cut off the head and bore it away triumphantly. At least I had one trophy to show for my night's vigil.

My second brush with a member of the cat family came when my Inspector told me that two members of the Malay Home Guard had been brought to the station, badly mauled by a leopardess in scrub land about two miles north-west of Jitra. I went into the office and saw the men—one with vicious wounds on his shoulders and arms while the other had deep claw marks on the back of his head.

They told me that they had found two leopard cubs at the edge of a small patch of rubber trees. Chasing after them they were able to catch hold of both. The leopardess had appeared like a bolt out of the blue, springing on one man and ripping him right down the back with her sharp claws. He dropped the cub, as did his companion when he grabbed for his rifle. The leopardess sprang again and as he grasped the firearm she landed on his back and sank her teeth deeply into his shoulder. He slewed the rifle round and fired, blowing a hole in her belly.

With the force of the shot the beast had dropped to the ground and run off into the scrub, part of her intestines trailing on the ground.

Settling the two men in a police truck I sent them off to the hospital in Alor Star, and taking four men with me, armed with Sten guns, I went to the spot where the beast had last been seen.

We had no difficulty in picking up the animal's trail. Dark blood stained the grass and mingled with the dust. For nearly one hundred yards we followed the tell-tale evidence until the blood disappeared into a dense thicket. The sound of deep, laboured breathing came from the centre and occasionally a deep gurgling sound, as blood welled up in the throat of the dying animal. The four policemen pointed their Stens in the direction of the sounds. I gently parted some of the branches and pushed the muzzle of my automatic shotgun through the opening.

The leopardess lay on the ground, gasping and choking, her once elegant spotted coat now stained with blood and caked in dust. I lost my grip on one of the branches and the sound of it whipping back made the animal turn its head. The cold slant eyes met mine and a snarl arose from the beast's throat. The leopardess tried to struggle to her feet to make an attack but I doubt if she would have been able to spring, because of her terrible wounds. I shot her through the heart and as she fell back, the snarl changed to a gurgle as the blood rushed out.

A scuffling sound came from the rear of the thicket as the two cubs fled. Although we hunted over a wide area we could find no trace of them and could only hope that they were strong enough to fend for themselves.

The policemen removed the animal's head and skinned it for me. Later the flesh was boiled off. The skull now stands, alongside that of the tigress, on a bookcase in my sitting-room—a constant reminder of a fearless mother who died protecting her young.

M

12

Shooting the Rapids

Upon successfully completing a course on Malayan law and language at the Kuala Kubu Police College, in March 1954 I was given the command of the No. 7 Police Field Force based at Kuantan in Pahang State—the town that was to gain immortality in both the book and the film of *A Town Like Alice* by Nevil Shute. The camp, surrounded by a high barbed-wire fence, was spread over a large area about two miles north of the town and, with the exception of two Malay inspectors, all the platoon commanders were British police lieutenants.

Many of these lieutenants were little older than twenty-one and in many European communities the snob element had the impertinence to look on them with disdain. They completely ignored them socially, treating these young men as if they were poor whites in the Southern States of America. The main reason for this apartheid was that the rank of lieutenant was ambiguous—it was not a commissioned grade but of equal status to an Asian inspector, which, in the eyes of snobs, classed them as social inferiors.

The lieutenants had a difficult job to do and, as is the lot of most junior grades, were called upon to undertake many of the more hazardous and difficult tasks. They did a fine job and invariably had small commands of their own, such as leading jungle patrols, directing operations from jungle forts and heading detachments of policemen guarding rubber estates. Only a mere handful managed to get hold of the occasional 'soft' job that came along, such as intelligence officer, transport officer or working in the Signals Division. The human mind works in strange ways. These lieutenants in the desk jobs were looked upon with greater tolerance by the snobbish Europeans than their counterparts who endured all the hardships of jungle life.

At Kuantan there were eight platoons consisting of over two hundred and fifty N.C.O.s and men, plus transport and signals sections and headquarters staff—bringing the total complement to well over three hundred. It took days of endless conferences and inspections of the countryside to familiarise myself with the terrain and the strength of the local terrorist organisation. At the operations conferences I had to listen to all sorts of ideas put forward by a variety of men, many of whom had never even heard a shot fired in anger, let alone been instrumental in pulling the trigger themselves. On the other hand some were highly experienced policemen and perhaps the most reliable of all was Bill Humble, the Special Branch officer for the Kuantan District. A former London Metropolitan detective, he was one of the most efficient men I ever had the privilege of meeting in Malaya. His intelligent methods of obtaining information and following up the leads that came as a result had culminated in many 'kills' being recorded against Communist bands in Pahang.

With a small bodyguard, I drove round the Kuantan District visiting the rubber estate managers—the most notable being a massive Scot, Jock Thomson, who looked after the plantations in Jabor Valley. Jock had to be tough to survive in this area—at least two police lieutenants and one assistant manager were killed on the road leading to the main inhabitated part of the estate. Many special constables died as well, their widows and children receiving little or no compensation from the Government or the companies who owned the rubber estates. This heartless treatment of the near relatives of the Malay policemen killed during the Emergency applied to every part of the country. Many men were killed protecting rubber estates but very seldom did the companies dip into their substantial profits to help the families left in a state of near poverty to mourn the loss of a father or son.

When I got out of my car outside Jock's magnificent house he greeted me as if I were a long-lost brother. He explained that, apart from his assistants and police lieutenant, mine was the first European face he had seen for several months. He immediately invited me to look over his house—a showpiece of modern comfort, with his one great pride being the floor of the lounge. Before entering he asked me to remove my shoes lest any scratches be made on the high polish which covered the dark brown wood. When he offered me a drink he led me to the verandah. All drinking was done in this part, he explained, for fear a glass might be broken scattering fragments on the precious lounge floor. Apart from this obsession with his home, Jock was a kind-hearted man, lavishing on me the best food and drink for the entire weekend. He did not forget my bodyguard and went to no end of trouble to ensure they were billeted in comfortable quarters and that the estate shop laid on a special treat for them.

The headquarters of the Pahang Consolidated Tin Company were also in the Kuantan District, thirty miles from town and deep in the jungle. There were three lines of communication to this highly organised complex: by road, on a small narrow-gauge railway, and by air. For inexplicable reasons the terrorists never attacked the road or the railway, but tried on many occasions to shoot down the light aircraft coming in to land at the tiny air strip gouged out from the heart of the dense jungle.

One of the more remote areas within the jurisdiction of No 7 Field Force was Fort Dixon, standing in mountainous territory one hundred and fifty miles from Kuantan. To reach it entailed a road journey of one hundred and twenty miles to Kuala Lipis, by boat up the mighty Pahang River, branching off to the north to follow a turbulent tributary, the Sungai Kechau, before coming to the aboriginal village inhabited by the Sakai tribe.

Fort Dixon had been built beside the village and every effort was being made to win over the aborigines to the side of the Security Forces. A great deal of success had been made in this direction.

I decided to spend some time at the fort and when the next platoon was due to change over with the one that had completed its monthly tour of duty, I travelled to Kuala Lipis with the lieutenant and his thirty men. Next morning at the small pier, two sturdily built boats, fitted with 10 h.p. outboard engines, were being loaded with ammunition, foodstuffs and other stores. Paddles were also provided, strapped to the insides of the boats in case of an engine breaking down. As I stood talking to the lieutenant, a colourfully dressed man walked up, swept the hat from his head and bowed in front of me.

He was about four feet six inches tall, but thickset, with a skin the colour of deep mahogany. The picture of sartorial elegance, he would have succeeded in putting any Carnaby Street mod to shame. He wore a pair of vivid yellow shoes, bright green drill trousers, a multi-hued shirt, with red the predominant colour, a broad blue tie, a white drill jacket and, to top the entire outfit, a small straw trilby with a red and yellow striped band running diagonally around it. A large watch was attached to his right wrist.

He glanced at the monster timepiece, held it to his ear, listening intently to the loud ticking, then said something in a language completely alien to me. I smiled at him and held up my hands to show I did not understand a word he was saying. He held up his hands in the same gesture, grinned widely, showing every tooth in his mouth, looked at his watch once more and walked off to join the men working on the boats.

I noticed that the lieutenant was almost doubled up with laughter and asked him if he knew the man. When he ceased to hold his sides he told me that our well-dressed friend was a member of the Sakai tribe, employed as a guide by the Commanding Officer at Fort Dixon. For this he was paid one and a half dollars a day (3s. 6d.). For months he had been saving up for a trip to Kuala Lipis and his appearance and behaviour had caused a senation in the small town. It had been the first time a Sakai had ventured near civilisation and, for almost the entire weekend, had spent most of his time going about the town, buying all the gayest clothes he could lay his hands on.

The loading operations completed, I got into the first boat with the platoon sergeant and we set off up the Pahang River. The waterway was broad and the current was slow and sluggish, vastly different from the Sungai Kechau. When, after two hours, we entered this river we found ourselves in a swift-flowing stream, bounded on either side by jungle and running through deep gorges hundreds of feet high. The outboard motor struggled gamely against the strength of the current. After about two miles of slow progress, we entered the first stretch of boiling, foaming, white-flecked water and the engine screamed its defiance as the boat was thrown and tossed by the force of a thousand demons suddenly unleashed.

From there onwards we were forced to crouch in the bottom of the boat, with one man nursing the engine and steering the course indicated by the second boatman, perched in the bow and looking ahead. All changes in course were given by hand as it was impossible to make oneself heard above the thunderous roar of the raging torrent. We dodged huge boulders rearing out of the foaming water, ducked under great branches of trees that almost touched the surface of the river, hugged the banks of deep channels and at times seemed hardly to be moving at all as the engine strained to its utmost capacity to get the boat through.

The fight went on for mile after mile. All the time we climbed higher and higher into the mountains with the river reaching what seemed to be great depths and becoming more turbulent as each mile passed. Now and again huge tree-trunks would flash past, thumping and crashing against the rocks, and being carried along as if they were no heavier than corks. Our boat was taking a tremendous amount of punishment and when I looked at the second craft bobbing and twisting in our wake, it seemed to be the height of madness to be attempting to negotiate such a river. Without any warning the water levelled off and we swept into a strong, firm current but without any signs of turbulence.

Our little friend had insisted on climbing into my boat when we left Kuala Lipis. As soon as we cast off he had removed all his finery until he was left wearing a tiny loin-cloth. The clothing had then been carefully rolled up and placed in a cheap fibre suitcase. Throughout the journey he sat clutching the suitcase up to his chest but now that the quieter waters had been reached he stood up, full of life again. Opening the case he pulled out his clothes and started to dress. He stood next to me and in the cramped space kept everyone amused as he tried to sort out the arms in the shirt and jacket. He had great difficulty with the trousers and when he seemed unable to make up his mind which was the front and the back, I offered to help. I finished by tying a knot in his tie. He was delighted and took up a position in the bow looking remarkably like a cockerel surveying his territory from the top of a fence post.

The reason for his fine array and posturing became obvious as we rounded the next bend in the river. The jungle had been cleared on both sides and on one bank was a long atap hut standing on stilts. At the river's edge stood a group of tiny men and women and children, shouting and waving their arms. Although they were his friends the little man in the bow completely ignored their cries of welcome, occasionally glancing their way with a look that denoted he considered them to be vastly inferior beings.

The crowd raced along the bank, keeping pace with the boats until we reached a makeshift jetty. Fort Dixon lay before us, spread out on the face of a hill that had been cleared of all jungle and undergrowth. The resident platoon, about to depart, were soon on the scene and the boats were unloaded.

The little man trotted away, surrounded by throngs of admirers, eager no doubt to hear of his travels and of how the other half lived.

A tall, gangling man, stripped to the waist and wearing only a pair of tattered shorts and jungle boots, shook my hand and introduced himself as Police Lieutenant Underwood. He had waived the normal monthly change-over and had been at Fort Dixon for six months without a break. He had been responsible for the constructional work on the large barrack buildings and the establishment of an excellent liaison with the aborigines. Lieutenant Underwood told me that he was feeling particularly sad. His tour of duty had expired and he was compelled to take six months' leave in Britain. This hard-working policeman loved the Sakai people and I was soon to discover that the feeling was mutual—they had a great deal of respect for him and greatly sorrowed his departure.

I was billeted in a hut at the top of the compound, with a commanding view of a vast area of jungle, which included some magnificent trees with tops reaching heights of two hundred feet. On many varieties the leaves were changing colour, prior to falling. When I looked across the wide canopy it appeared like some giant painting made up of greens, yellows, purples, browns and reds. The crowning glory was the flame of the forest, with masses of huge red flowers adorning the branches.

A double barbed-wire fence ringed the fort, with numerous look-out towers, and at the top of the hill an air strip had been built providing sufficient landing space for a single-engined Pionair. They were marvellous small aircraft, only requiring one hundred yards for landing and take-off, and did useful work while helicopters were in short supply throughout Malaya.

The day after my arrival I went down to the store to meet

the chief of the tribe, who went by the name of Tupai. He was a sturdy little fellow, about four feet three inches tall. With the aid of a Malay constable, who could speak a little of the Sakai dialect, he welcomed me to his village and showed me round the fort's store, in which he spent a good deal of time. A variety of goods were on display, ranging from salt, sugar, tea and cigarettes to an assortment of cheap trinkets.

He told me his tribe existed from the proceeds of hunting expeditions in which the only weapon used was a blowpipe and invited me to go along on one of their trips.

I went with the villagers on a couple of occasions and was amazed by the deadly accuracy they achieved with those silent, lethal weapons. The blowpipes were of various sizes, some as long as eight feet, and fired short arrows made from bamboo slivers, sharpened to a needle point, and dipped in a poison obtained from the bark of a tree. The potency of the poison varied, depending on the size of the creature being pursued.

The range of the blowpipe was limited but, in the hands of an expert, a bird the size of a sparrow could be brought down at twenty-five yards. Considering the density of the jungle it was very seldom that a target was visible beyond this distance. As the dart was fired, the only sound that could be heard was a low *phut* made by the exhalation of air through the lips compressed on the mouthpiece. Both the blowpipes and the arrows were the work of fine craftsmen, the pipe being made of one piece of bamboo, bored through at the joints. A hollow reed was then inserted along the entire length, giving the same sort of glossy finish as the interior of the barrel in a smooth-bore gun.

The Sakais were also experts in snaring and trapping wild animals, such as wild boar and the larger species of deer. There was certainly never any chance that they would run short of food as the region was a paradise abounding in wild life, especially as far as birds were concerned. During the many days of patrolling I saw wild peacocks, jungle fowl, with the cocks clad in rainbow-coloured raiment, flycatchers of every hue, some with tails four or five times longer than their bodies, ugly hornbills, with huge beaks that made me wonder how on earth they could support them, let alone fly, and scores of other varieties, both large and small.

I had been told of the tracking abilities of the tribe and on my first patrol asked the Sakai, via my interpreter, to inform me of any footprints or tracks he might see. The floor of the jungle was a solid mat of leaves, in places up to a foot deep, but the tracker stopped on several occasions, saying he had detected the marks of a wild pig. I could see the faint depression in the bed of leaves, but it bore no resemblance to the footprint of any living creature. I expressed my doubt and the poor Sakai looked extremely hurt. He then bared about six layers of leaves and only then was I able to see the clear-cut print.

I had also been told about their ability to move silently through the jungle and decided to test this too. We reached some massive trees, which had shed most of their leaves— huge affairs about the size of rhubarb leaves and dry and brittle to touch. To stand on one produced a sharp noise, similar to the cracking of a branch. Apart from some scrub bushes, scattered around in odd clumps, there was no place offering any real measure of concealment. I instructed the Sakai to search an area of the forest about five hundred yards away and to return as quietly as he could.

With the seven Malays in the squad I sat down at the base of a tree and lit a cigarette. After fifteen minutes I expected to hear rustling noises or the cracking of the bone-dry leaves, giving notice of the tracker's return. But try as hard as I might I could hear no suspicious sounds. Only birds squawked and insects hummed. Another fifteen minutes went by and from a bush only three feet from where I sat, the grinning face of the Sakai looked out. He said he had been hiding in the bush watching us for some time. After this masterly display I was glad that these remarkable little men were on our side.

The Sakai women were slightly smaller than the menfolk and always went about naked from the waist up, their only garment being a small loincloth or the briefest of skirts, made from tree bark. Religion of any denomination had not touched them and they had few fears or superstitions. Their only dread was thunder and lightning and at the first signs of the approach of a storm they would huddle together in the longhouse and stay there until it had passed over. The longhouse was home to the entire village, with everyone cooking, eating, sleeping, making love, raising children and dying under one roof.

Shortly before my two-week stay at Fort Dixon came to an end, I was invited, along with Underwood and several other Malays, to the longhouse for a mekan besar (feast). When we arrived the entire tribe was there to greet us, with Tupai and his senior male members in the forefront of the throng. There was a good deal of bowing and handshaking before Tupai ushered us into the longhouse. When I ducked through the low entrance and entered, I was nearly choked by the dense smoke that swirled lazily around the interior like a bank of fog. A fire burned brightly in the middle of the floor—the smoke being allowed to find its own way out, unaided, through the door, the atap roof and the few apertures which represented windows.

Tupai explained that the smoke was needed to keep out the mosquitoes and sandflies. After several minutes of coughing and spluttering in the fume-laden atmosphere I found myself growing used to it and as the night wore on the smoke ceased to bother me.

Masses of huge plantain leaves lay on the floor, covered with an alarming quantity of food. There was rice, grown on the hillside, bamboo shoots and other edible roots, wild fruits of all kinds, fish freshly caught from the teeming river, roast wild pig, venison, small birds of various species, roasted in the glowing embers of the fire, and finally several platters bearing round pieces of meat. We sat cross-legged on the floor around this magnificent banquet and I asked the Malay next to me what animal had produced the peculiarly shaped pieces of meat.

'No animal, tuan,' he said with a big grin, 'that is snake meat.'

I stayed well clear of the snake but did justice to the remainder, which was delicious. There seemed no end to the meal or to the bowls of tea handed round from time to time and made from leaves given to the Sakais by one of our storemen.

As the last morsels were being cleaned away the chief's wife, who throughout the meal had stayed with the rest of the women in another part of the longhouse, arrived holding a large plantain leaf. She bent down beside me and Tupai instructed me to partake of the delicacy which had been specially prepared for the occasion. My stomach turned over and my gorge rose as I gazed at the platter only inches from my face and watched hundreds of the fattest maggots I have ever seen squirming and wriggling on the broad, green leaf. Without appearing to be rude, I declined, saying that I had already eaten too much.

Tupai smiled all over his old wizened face, reached over and selected one of the largest. Popping it in his mouth, he chewed for several seconds then swallowed, washing the repulsive creature down his throat with a mouthful of tea. As we sat talking he dipped into the dish from time to time, eating the maggots as one eats potato crisps when having a drink.

My journey back to Kuala Lipis was just as hair-raising as the trip upstream had been and for most of the way the outboard was in reverse as we shot the rapids. The worst stage of all was the drop down from the mountains when the river bent sharply away at right angles to the downwards course, before levelling off. The stream was split at this point by a reef, sticking out of the water and flanked on the downward side by a similar formation on the bank.

As we reached the bend the boatman hauled his craft round and almost succeeded in tipping it over. The side grated and tore along the reef in the centre of the river and the boat keeled over in the opposite direction. We would have been powerless to prevent the craft capsizing, due to the force of the water, had it chosen to do so. However, after wobbling dangerously, with the bows rising out of the stream and crashing down again in a cloud of spray, it steadied up and we found ourselves in more placid water.

As we chugged along and I wiped the sweat from my brow the boatman told me that on two occasions boats had been wrecked at the very same spot on the bend. Seven men had been drowned and a considerable quantity of firearms lost.

Two months later I paid another visit to Fort Dixon and after stepping ashore at Kuala Lipis, on my return, I vowed I would never shoot the rapids again if I could possibly avoid it. For that matter, I would not expect my men to do it either. It took three weeks of writing letters, sending signals and attending numerous conferences before official sanction was given for the provision of helicopters to carry men in and out of the fort whenever the platoons were changed over.

13

Snakes Alive!

O<small>NE</small> of the bravest Asian policemen who served with me was a young Indian inspector called Ramuddin. Fear had no meaning as far as he was concerned and, although some were inclined to put his exploits down to sheer foolishness, I always considered him to be a highly courageous and competent police officer.

Terrorist incidents were on the wane with the Security Forces well organised and highly mobile and our main job at Kuantan was to try to prevent food supplies from reaching the bandits and thus hasten their surrender. We laid numerous ambushes on the outskirts of the town and caught scores of sympathisers, from teenage youths and girls to some elderly Chinese who had always been highly respected members of the community. After a month of intensive work our operations began to pay dividends and over a period of several days eight terrorists stumbled out of the jungle and surrendered at police road blocks at various points on the main highway.

They were thin and emaciated, their clothing in rags and their bodies a mass of sores brought about by insect bites and cuts, which had received no medical attention. One man pleaded for food, gasping that he had not eaten for nearly two weeks. They were taken to hospital, where their wounds were treated, and in small amounts were introduced to food once again. When interrogated they said there was only about one dozen of their band left in the mountains and it was highly unlikely they would ever surrender because they were hardened members of the Communist movement.

At this time a scheme had been introduced where former terrorists who surrendered were given the opportunity of joining killer squads, formed to track down the men who had previously fought with them. It was found that there was little love lost between those who belonged to the terrorist organisation, as it was held together mainly by fear of reprisals from other members. Executions of erring terrorists within the various sections were quite common.

When the eight terrorists had fully recovered they agreed to join one of these squads, saying they would gladly lead the police to where their companions were hidden. Inspector Ramuddin was given the job of leading them and with four constables and the eight former terrorists set off for the Communists' camp situated about three miles south of the main road. A well-concealed path, which previously had been unknown to the police, was used to get into the jungle. Eventually the main path branched off into what was little more than a tunnel through the dense undergrowth. When they had crawled and stumbled over tree-roots and rocks for about a mile, one of the informers stopped the inspector and warned him that the camp lay only two hundred yards ahead.

Inspector Ramuddin took one of the former terrorists with him and instructed the remainder of the squad to set up an ambush. To have led the entire squad to the camp would have been too noisy. Carrying a revolver and a Sten gun, he moved forward, followed by the former terrorist, armed with a Sten.

The sound of voices speaking in Chinese floated towards them as they emerged from the deep scrub and into a patch of thick vegetation. The path led round the base of a tree and disappeared between two bushes. Crawling on their stomachs the two men edged forward, inch by inch, waiting for the moment when the quick snap of a twig would warn the terrorists that danger was near. But they made it and now the voices were clear and distinct, only several yards away.

The inspector made an opening in the foliage and looked into the small clearing. Two bashas had been erected under a couple of trees and five Chinese squatted round a rusty bucket eating cold rice, which they must have had stored for some time judging by the condition of the container. Their rifles lay in the grass within easy reach. The inspector and his former terrorist ally lay watching for about five minutes, trying to ascertain whether or not other men were present in the vicinity. The five men talked loudly to each other as they packed the rice into their mouths with their bare hands.

Satisfied that the five men were alone, Inspector Ramuddin sprang to his feet and burst through the bushes into the clearing. The terrorists, with mixed looks of terror and shock, leaped to their feet, but were unable to reach their rifles before being cut down by a spray of bullets coming from the inspector's Sten, which he held at waist-level. Three men fell to the ground while the others took a leap into the bushes with the bullets from the informer's Sten thudding into the foliage behind them.

Two of the fallen men were dead, with bullets through the heart and head, while the other lay writhing in pain, clutching a hole in the right side of his chest. Attracted by the sound of shots, the rest of the squad ran into the clearing and set off in pursuit of the two men who had escaped. A quick search revealed no trace of them and the inspector decided to return to Kuantan. Without any feeling of remorse for their former comrades the informers in the squad pulled out two poles supporting the bashas and tied the dead men to them by their hands and feet.

The terrorist's chest wound was bandaged by a constable and he was placed on a makeshift stretcher. Using a fast route through the jungle, the procession reached the road and linked up with the police truck positioned for their return. Before they reached Kuantan the wounded terrorist died; it proved impossible to staunch the flow of blood from the gaping gash in his chest. Two days later the two men who had escaped death in the clearing got on to the main road and stopped the first police vehicle that came along—to surrender.

They too, had titbits of information to offer and assured the Special Branch officer who handled the interrogation that the remainder of the gang were going to attempt to contact several of the Chinese squatter families living around Kuantan. Supplies of food were desperately needed and it was thought that some of the families would be willing to help the bandits.

Due to the amount of territory to be covered, the Field Force were asked to assist in the operation to trap the guerillas and I selected a dozen men and paired them off with members of the killer squad. I teamed up with Inspector Ramuddin.

At dusk we drove along the bumpy road to Kampong Padang and jumped off the slow-moving truck just round the corner from the house we intended to watch. Quietly, we moved along a path through the tall lallang that partially screened the building on three sides. The point where the terrorists were most likely to emerge from the jungle lay at the rear of the house. We both wanted first chance to watch it.

'I'll toss you for it,' I said to the inspector.

'All right,' he replied, 'I've got a twenty piece ... somewhere in my pockets.'

He groped in the pockets of his jungle-green trousers and after a considerable search found the coin, trapped in a seam.

'Heads I take the rear,' I said, as he flicked the coin into the air.

When it came down he failed to catch hold of it and it dropped into the grass. By now it was almost completely dark and there was no moon to ease the utter blackness of the jungle. On our hands and knees we searched around for

N

almost a minute before he called out that he had found the coin.

'I've won,' he said in a triumphant whisper. I peered at the tiny silver coin trapped by the grass. It was reverse side up.

Inspector Ramuddin worked his way round to the rear and I took up my position farther along the path at the side nearest the thick cover. We arranged our vantage points within hailing distance of each other, but in such a way that if we both opened fire we would not hit the other's position.

As I settled down to wait, my eyes grew accustomed to the darkness and I was able to see the outline of the house not far from where I stood. In selected positions in a wide semicircle around the building the rest of the killer squad waited, listening and watching. Occasionally someone coughed inside the house and after about an hour I heard loud snoring—at least one member of the family had settled down for the night. The time dragged slowly past: seven o'clock ... eight ... nine ... ten—and then the shot rang out, followed by a shout.

It came from Inspector Ramuddin's position and I quickly moved forward to join him. As I raced through the lallang a small man darted between us and tried to get over the fence that surrounded the house. Almost simultaneously our automatic shotguns cracked out and he slumped sideways on to the ground, shot in the side and one arm.

He was on his feet again before we had time to move and, finding the fence too difficult to climb, turned to face us. As he shouted an obscenity his hands went to the grenades tied to his belt.

The inspector had him in his sights instantly and fired four more shots into the terrorist's body. In the final moments of death the guerilla scrabbled for the grenades but it was only seconds before he pitched backwards to impale himself on the strands of barbed wire on the fence. He was dead by the time we reached him, his body almost cut in half by the heavy bullets.

Now that shots had been fired it was pointless continuing with the ambush plans. Swiftly, we completely surrounded the house and the inspector and I went up to the back door. No one answered our heavy knocking. The door, a frail affair, was locked. Throwing our combined weight on it we forced the lock and burst into a small room. Four Chinese crouched in a corner: an old man, obviously the grandfather, a woman of about seventy who appeared to be his wife and two younger people in their thirties—man and wife. We searched all through the house while the family protested that they hated the Communists—the young man continually getting in my way as I looked in cupboards and boxes in an unused room at the front.

When nothing was found we turned our attention to the ground at the rear, between the house and the fence. It only took five minutes to uncover a small drum containing rice and dried fish, hidden under a bundle of cut lallang about eight feet from the fence. At first the family said they knew nothing . . . they had not planted the drum themselves. Some of their neighbours were obviously trying to get them into trouble, they maintained.

I told them bluntly that if no one talked I would have to take them to Kuantan where they would all be locked up. At this the young woman began to cry and her husband tried to comfort her. When she became hysterical he straightened up and admitted that he had planted the food in the garden.

'My wife knows nothing of this,' he told me, 'and the old people are innocent. I have been giving food to the men in the jungle for some time. Take me—but leave them alone.'

We left the old couple in the house, but took the man and his wife out to the road and placed them in a vehicle that had been summoned as a result of a wireless message. For most of the next day they were questioned by Special Branch officers and when it was all over a comprehensive picture was obtained of how the guerillas were being supplied with food. The woman denied all knowledge of aiding the terrorists and could not be trapped by skilful questioning. Early in the evening she was freed, leaving her husband, who had made a full confession, to face the serious charges of aiding and abetting the Communists.

With the remnants of the gang still in the area I made a reconnaissance flight in a small aircraft, piloted by an army sergeant, over the top and around the slopes of Gunong Serudom. This search revealed a man-made clearing beside an almost dried-up watershed, and although I was not convinced that the area could contain a hide-out, felt obliged to investigate with a platoon.

Next day we set off and prepared a small base camp beside a stream trickling through the foothills. A good night's rest and we were up at dawn to split up into groups of five, in order to search the area as thoroughly as possible. Taking four men with me I set a compass course for the spot I had pin-pointed on the map.

As we broke through the dense undergrowth we found ourselves walking between massive trees, surrounded by thick layers of fallen leaves, each one playing host to countless leeches. They clung tenaciously to our boots and climbed on to our clothing, finding their way through the smallest tears in the cloth. No pain was felt when they sucked the blood—the first we knew of their presence on our bodies was when these disgusting creatures were touched. When we stopped for a rest, after walking through the area for nearly an hour, I picked off more than thirty from my arms, legs, face and neck. Even to think of leeches is enough to send a shudder down my spine—they must surely be the most loathsome of all jungle life.

We reached the watershed and searched along the rim. Where the dried-up gorge levelled out a bit I found the spot I had seen from the air—a small clearing at the edge of the forest. A crude shelter on stilts, which judging from its dilapidated appearance had not been used for several months, stood in one corner. There were no other signs of life. At this point we were almost three thousand feet up the mountain and I decided to retrace our steps to the camp, this time following the watershed in order to see if there were any other signs of human habitation, either past or present.

Before long we were fighting and hacking our way through thickets of bamboo and thick creepers and having our faces, hands and clothing ripped and torn by the hair thorns that laced their way through the undergrowth. When the barriers grew thicker and the going got much tougher, we left the jungle and made our way down the centre of the watershed. I led the way, taking care not to repeat the accident on Gunong Perak, edging myself carefully from shelf to shelf of rock.

The first obstacle presented itself in the shape of a steep drop of around ten feet down on to a rocky ledge. I handed my .300 carbine to one of the constables and, sliding over the top ledge, dropped down on to the rock. As I landed I crouched forward on to my knees in order to gain a better grip, and found myself looking into a cavity in the side of the face. Two huge king cobras, in the process of rearing their heads, with their bodies coiling at the same time, stared back at me. They had, no doubt, been fast asleep in their warm crevice when the noise of my landing on the ledge had awakened them with a sharp shock. Sensing danger, they were ready to strike. Without a thought as to the depth of the drop, I launched myself into space, with a yell that caused a great deal of confusion among the members of the platoon.

Fortunately it was only six feet to the next ledge and I landed in a heap, arms and legs sprawled in a variety of directions. Shouting to the Malays to get out of the watershed I got to my feet and scrambled up the side. I lay in the undergrowth getting my breath back after the fierce exertion. When the platoon joined me they were eager to find out the reason for my strange performance on the two ledges. When I told them about the cobras, one remarked cheerily that he had seen a man die within minutes of being bitten by such a snake. His words were cold comfort.

We spent two more days combing the other side of the mountain but neither traces of camps nor terrorists were found. For several weeks afterwards we searched wide areas of jungle and tightened our grip on the food suppliers. Starved, ill and close to death, nine guerillas gave themselves up in the course of a few days and when interrogated we were satisfied that at least one more section of the Communist movement had been hunted down and finally routed.

Inspector Ramuddin, whom I got to know well and respect a great deal, was to die needlessly and tragically several months later, while at the peak of his youth and fame.

Information was received that there was a Communist camp near Gambang, a semi-deserted village on the main east–west road through Pahang. The Hussars, who were on patrol duty on the roads in this area, were requested to mortar the position, as it was practically impossible to approach it on foot without being spotted. The mortar squad was dropped off at a concealed spot on the road and the transport continued on its way, in order to allay suspicion should anyone see the troops. Inspector Ramuddin and his killer squad moved into position about three hundred yards from where the camp was believed to be situated and awaited the start of the mortar barrage. The Hussars moved into position, accompanied by a police lieutenant who was to pin-point the target area.

Scores of shells were lobbed into the region for almost fifteen minutes until the firing was interrupted by the sight of one of the killer squad standing on top of a mound, waving his arms and shouting for someone to join him. The lieutenant ran over and was led to a spot at the edge of the area which had been most severely hit by the shell-fire. Inspector Ramuddin lay on the ground, a wound the size of a man's fist in his side, where a shell fragment had penetrated.

He was rushed to Kuantan Hospital, where an emergency

operation was carried out. But his injuries were too grave and he died as they wheeled him from the theatre. An air of gloom hung over the camp for days. Death was never far from any of us and was regarded as an inevitable part of our job, but the killing of this brave lad shocked us all. Due to his courage and devotion to duty, he had a special place in our hearts. But on this occasion he had been too impetuous and when the shelling started had moved into the target area too quickly.

Ironically, no trace of a terrorist camp was found at Gambang and, although the district was subjected to an intensive search, no guerillas came to light.

While visiting a police station near Kuantan one day to check on a report of some slight terrorist activity in the area a crowd of Malays entered the backyard, pushing a hand-cart. My eyes nearly popped out of my head when I saw the cargo, tied securely to the woodwork—a large croco-dile. With the sergeant I hurried out and found that the creature was very much alive. Its jaws were firmly bound together, as were the front and back legs. The tail was also lashed—to a pole which extended well behind the cart.

One man spoke up and said that the crocodile had been captured in a deep pool in a nearby river. It had been there for a number of years and had not caused any trouble until several days previously when it had almost succeeded in snatching a village woman as she washed some clothes in the river. To capture it they had slaughtered a goat and left it to decompose for several days. A long piece of rotan, a jungle creeper that hangs down from the tops of large trees and has more strength in it than the average stout rope, was cut. A large steel hook was then attached to one end and inserted into the goat. The bait was lowered into the pool and a double turn made in the rotan, around a stout tree.

With the rotting goat, an extreme delicacy for crocodiles, dangling above the reptile's lair, it could not resist the temptation. Barely an hour passed before the villagers saw the rotan running out into the depths of the pool and after a short time the crocodile came to the surface, threshing around in an effort to free itself from the hook embedded in its lower jaw. After a further hour of frantic struggling it sank into the black water, completely exhausted.

Several of the Malays swam out, clutching three lengths of thinner rotan, and lashed the reptile's jaws and feet together. It required almost the entire manpower of the village to haul the great beast out of the water—it must have weighed around six hundred pounds. A handcart was borrowed and the creature ceremoniously wheeled to the police station, for disposal. The local policemen did not want to have anything to do with the beast and protested to the villagers that they take the offending crocodile away and get rid of it elsewhere.

Throughout the heated discussion that went on behind the police station with voices being raised on either side, the crocodile stared at the mob surrounding it, with its two small evil-looking eyes. Occasionally it gave a twitch as it tried to free itself from the lashings, but although the cart wobbled and nearly fell over, the creature remained held fast.

After a time it appeared that the villagers intended to walk off and leave the crocodile with the police. Several men drifted away, shouting on their companions to follow them. It was at this point that a young Malay constable, standing in the background and taking no part in the argument, mentioned that he knew of an old Chinese shopkeeper who might be interested in the creature. The sergeant breathed a sigh of relief and sent the policeman to find the man.

Half an hour later he returned, accompanied by a thin-looking Chinese of around seventy, with a wrinkled face and wispy beard, shuffling along behind him. I saw his eyes light up when he saw the immense size of the crocodile. The villagers hung back as the old man walked round and round the cart, prodding the reptile with a stick as a farmer inspects cattle prior to buying at a market. Three times round the handcart and he was satisfied. He would give ten dollars (about £1 5s.) for the crocodile, on condition that the men wheeled it to his shop.

The villagers agreed on the spot and the policemen were only too keen to lend a hand to remove it from the precincts of the station. The old man handed over two five-dollar notes and shuffled off. His crocodile, obviously destined to be turned into handbags, wallets and shoes, followed behind, surrounded by a crowd of men, all smiles and joking together, well satisfied now that their respective problems had been solved.

Prior to his departure from Malaya in 1954, General Templer carried out a farewell tour of the country. Along with Ernest Duval, a police depot officer, I was assigned to accompany the High Commissioner on part of his journey as personal bodyguard. Every possible precaution, involving some of the tightest security that Malaya had ever seen, was taken to ensure that nothing untoward happened to him. Due to his relentless prosecution of the war against the terrorists, General Templer had made many enemies, in various cross-sections of the public, and throughout the tour both he and Lady Templer seemed tense and highly strung, although they drove themselves on untiringly through a host of social engagements.

Nevertheless it was impossible not to be captivated by his dynamic personality and quick sense of humour. On one occasion while walking down the stairs in the residence of the British Adviser to Kedah, he stopped, turned to Ernest and me and remarked: 'Gentlemen, they have been very discreet in the selection of my bodyguard. No one would ever believe you were policemen.' His eyebrows raised as he smiled and he turned to walk on.

He had indeed been joking—both Ernest and I were of the same physique: five foot eleven inches tall, forty-six inches around the chest and weighing around fifteen stone. Apart from these features it was impossible to disguise the bulge under our jackets, just under the left arm, where a heavy revolver nestled in its leather shoulder holster.

A similar spell of duty came my way when in October 1956 the Duke of Edinburgh visited Kuala Lumpur while on his way from Britain to Australia to perform the opening ceremony of the British Commonwealth Games. He had a vast number of functions to attend during his two-day visit, but carried them out with an air of genuine charm which left a lasting impression among those he met.

One souvenir I wished to take back to Britain when the time eventually came for me to return was the skin of a python. As a boy, I had always been fascinated by drawings and photographs of this large snake and enthralled by the sheer beauty of the exquisite markings on its skin. When a friend gave me the name and address of a Japanese taxidermist in Singapore, renowned for his work with snake skins, I felt the time had come to get a hold of one. Finding one was no problem, but local knowledge informed me that in order to preserve the lustre of the skin, it had to be removed while the snake was still alive.

I passed the message round the kampongs that I was interested in obtaining a good specimen. Eventually a tapper from a nearby plantation turned up at my headquarters with the news that he had seen a very large python, sleeping in a patch of lallang, not far from the group of rubber trees from which he had been gathering latex. With four constables and the tapper eagerly leading the way, I went to the plantation.

As we warily approached the lallang the tapper put his finger to his lips, motioning us to be quiet. Several feet from where the python lay we halted and prepared our do-it-yourself snake-capturing equipment. This consisted of a long piece of strong rope with a loop on one end and fastened to a stout pole. The remainder of the rope was coiled up in one hand while with the other the pole was grasped, some way up from the base.

Everything in order, I took the pole and rope and moved forward. I was only several feet away from the great snake when I stepped on a twig. The python's head shot out from the mass of coils that was its body. It saw me instantly and started to slither away. As its body unfurled I saw a huge bulge in its midriff—we had disturbed it in the middle of digesting some large creature, which had been its last meal.

I ran in front of the python and tried to get the loop over its head, but the reptile would have none of it and kept striking out at the rope. Each time I missed, the loop had to be reopened. While this was being done the python took the opportunity of slipping away for a few more feet. This pantomime went on for more than ten minutes, with the constables shouting, cheering and dancing around the snake in an effort to head it away from the deep bushes.

As they grew happier so I became more frustrated. I tried a feint to one side and when the reptile struck out, withdrew the loop before it could make contact, then quickly lunged again and it head was firmly in the noose. The constables and the tapper fell in behind me and I dropped the pole. We started to haul on the rope. It was like some farcical tug-of-war, with the huge snake pulling in one direction and six heavily perspiring men hauling in the other. I wanted to get the reptile well out into the open, away from the small scrub trees, as I had been informed that a python was virtually harmless so long as he had no object on which to anchor his tail.

The tail end swished around, searching for an anchorage, and we pulled ever harder. We were making good, although slow, progress towards the open ground when, without warning, the tail made contact with a tree stump protruding from the lallang. In a flash the python whipped a loop round the object and arched its body backwards.

Before we knew what was happening we were flying through the air towards it, lifted off the ground by a swift and massive pull. I landed in a heap, about two feet from its body, and the rest of the men were scattered around like rag dolls on either side. Before the snake had time to get round me, I rolled away out of reach of its twisting frame. Fortunately the rope still remained firmly fixed around its neck. Picking ourselves up, we continued with the tug-of-war.

With the aid of the discarded pole the python's tail was levered off the stump and after a considerable struggle it lay in the lallang, well away from the trees. By this time six other rubber tappers had arrived on the scene, attracted by the commotion. With the pressure off the rope the snake seemed content to rest and one of the newly arrived men ran back to the trees and cut a large sapling, to which the python would have to be attached for skinning purposes.

When he returned with a slender sapling, the men quickly trimmed off the branches and once more we approached the snake. Its body threshed around all over the place as we tried to pin it to the ground. While four men held on to the rope the rest of us—eight in all—lunged and jumped trying to get hold of the reptile. Now and again we made contact but there was still plenty of power in the slithering body and it wriggled out of the way. Eventually the four men holding the rope threw it down and joined in. The extra weight made all the difference and with a good deal of shouting, laughing and cursing, the reptile was secured to the entire length of the sapling.

When all this was done I could not fathom out how on earth one could skin a live python when it was trussed up like a chicken with a mass of ropes around its body.

With a sharp knife I killed the reptile with a blow through the brain and when the final convulsions subsided we removed the rope. It was a relatively simple matter to remove the skin—once it was cut round behind the head, the whole thing peeled off as easily as the skin is pulled from a banana.

I was curious to find out more about the lump in its stomach and, when the flesh was cut open, it revealed a well grown young wild pig. Every bone in its body had been crushed.

The rubber tappers returned to their work and I set off with the constables, carrying the 19 ft. long skin over our shoulders as one carries a rolled-up carpet. At my bungalow I nailed it to the trunk of a fallen palm tree, in order to let the ants clean off the surplus flesh, which still adhered to the inside.

Next morning I found that they had done a most efficient job. Not only had they devoured the flesh, but had eaten almost half the skin as well. What did remain was riddled with holes . . . and utterly useless.

14

Finale

In March 1957, with full independence for Malaya lying just over the horizon, I was given the opportunity of staying on in the force or returning to Britain. The Malayan Government's policy with regard to the police after independence was to have as many of the senior posts occupied by Asians as possible. However, in common with a number of fellow officers, I was asked if I would care to stay and assist with the change-over.

I loved Malaya, having many good friends in all walks of life throughout the country, but in the days I pondered over the problem I found my thoughts flitting back to the life I had led in the open air as a youth on my beloved Deeside. I was now forty-five years of age and perhaps I felt myself growing that little bit older. The visions that filled my mind, of fishing for salmon, of hunting and of simply walking in the crystal-clear mountain air once again, began to suppress the spirit of adventure that still trickled faintly through my veins. I chose to return and I have never had cause to regret the decision.

Only once, several months after I settled in Scotland, did the wanderlust break over me. Feeling restless I wrote to the Colonial Office and requested a list of vacancies for police officers in the remaining colonies. When it arrived I read through it eagerly and found one that took my fancy— one British officer to take charge of the native police in the

Seychelles, in the Indian Ocean. Although the letter of application was started it was destined never to be posted.

Several days later I met Mary Marshall, the woman who was to change my entire outlook and bring to me a better understanding of life. Within a year we were married and my life turned a complete circle. I was back in Aboyne.

At Glentanar I soon found peace and contentment—things I had not given much thought to during the twenty-five years I had been away. I found them first as a salmon-fishing ghillie, then later, in addition to this work, roaming the pine forests and purple-clad hills in pursuit of red deer, woodcock, pheasant, grouse and that monarch among birds—the capercaillie.

My daily companions, as I go about my tasks, are the eagles that soar over the mountains and the rabbits and hares that forage for food in the fields and deep glens that cut through the rugged hills. The biggest killers that face my gun now are the wildcats, probably the most savage and remote of all creatures in Britain, living deep in the forests or rocky terrain, far from human ken. The biggest measure up to thirty-eight inches from tip of tail to nose and can top the scales at sixteen pounds.

When I return home in the evenings to my wife and two wonderful children, Allan and Susan, a young honey who can twist me round her little finger when she wants something, and we talk of the daily happenings in the ever-changing countryside, I find it hard to imagine that I was ever able to enjoy my other life—the years in which domesticity played no part.

And so the prophecies of the Siamese Buddhist priest, my fellow travelling companion in north Malaya, have come true—at least in the first two stages.

I have survived the two serious accidents—the second occurring in Aberdeenshire, not long after my return from the Far East, when a car in which I was travelling as a passenger skidded and crashed into a stone wall. I was knocked unconscious, severely bruised and had to have a considerable number of stitches inserted in a nasty gash on my head.

Again, as foretold, my wife and two children are with me.

Only the third prophecy remains unfulfilled—the one I will not be able to write about: my peaceful death at a ripe old age.